# One-Minute DISCIPLINE

## Classroom Management Strategies That Work

## By ARNIE BIANCO

Illustrated by Jeffrey Short

JOSSEY-BASS
A Wiley Company
www.josseybass.com

Published by Jossey-Bass
A Wiley Imprint
989 Market Street, San Francisco, CA 94103-1741    www.josseybass.com

Jossey-Bass books and products are available through most bookstores. To contact Jossey-Bass directly call our Customer Care Department within the U.S. at (800) 956-7739, outside the U.S. at (317) 572-3986 or fax (317) 572-4002.

Jossey-Bass also publishes its books in a variety of electronic formats. Some content that appears in print may not be available in electronic books.

**Library of Congress Cataloging-in-Publication Data**
Bianco, Arnie.
    One-minute discipline : classroom management techniques that work / Arnie Bianco.
        p. cm.
    Includes bibliographical references.
    ISBN 0-13-045298-X
        1. Classroom management—Handbooks, manuals, etc. 2. Teacher effectiveness—Handbooks, manuals, etc. I. Title.
    LB3013.B53 2002
    371.102'4—dc21                                                          2002023403

Printed in the United States of America
FIRST EDITION
PB Printing 20  19  18  17  16  15  14  13  12  11

*To Debbie:*

*My cheerleader,*

*my stepping stone,*

*and my love.*

# About the Author

Arnie Bianco (B.S., State University of New York, Geneseo, and M.Ed., University of Arizona, Tucson) taught for nine years at several grade levels and was a school principal for 24 years. He currently owns and directs a children and teen theatre in Tucson, and has been an adjunct instructor and student teacher supervisor at Chapman University for the past 15 years. Arnie also conducts One-Minute Discipline Workshops for teachers. He can be contacted by writing to 4475 N. Summerset Dr., Tucson, Arizona 85750.

# About This Teacher's Resource

*One-Minute Discipline* is a collection of over 100 techniques, strategies, and support ideas that will assist teachers in managing classroom behavior and promoting learning.

The one-minute ideas are complemented by relevant, fun illustrations and a simple-to-use format. You are shown:

*What* the strategy, technique, or idea is.

*Why* the teacher needs it.

*How* the teacher makes it work.

For quick reference and easy use, the materials are organized into ten sections focusing on various areas of the teacher's job. This book is printed in an 8¼ × 11 format that lays flat for photocopying of the reproducible forms, quotations, and other aids included. Here's an overview of the practical help you'll find in each section:

- Section 1, "Philosophy," provides a philosophical framework for the techniques and strategies presented in this resource, including a "Teacher Self-Check" to help monitor your own state of mind and outlook as the year progresses.

- Section 2, "Know Your Clients," features techniques and surveys, such as a "Classroom Atmosphere Survey," to assist you in learning more about your students and meeting their various individual needs.

- Section 3, "Home and School," presents ideas for promoting positive home–school communication, such as "Newsletters" and "Parent Homework Letter" as well as a "Parent Conference Checklist" and strategies for dealing with angry parents.

- Section 4, "The First Week of School," offers practical information and tips for getting the new year off to a good start, including a "Classroom Rules Check-list" that establishes order early in the year and prevents problem situations from occurring.

- Section 5, "Vocabulary," features techniques, quotations, and expressions that will help improve your skills when dealing with behavior problems, such as

"Baci di Tutti Bocci" ("kiss of all kisses"); responding to a broken rule or inappropriate behavior in an unemotional way; and motivating students with "Grandma's Law," a payoff ("dessert") when they complete a task.

- Section 6, "Techniques, Strategies, and Good Ideas," is packed with easy-to-use ideas that will increase your skill in handling particular behavior problems, such as "Noise-Level Control," a visual indicator of the acceptable talking level for each activity; "Private (Direct) Appeal," a technique that removes the culprit from his or her audience; and "Ask a Question, Pay a Chip," a technique for handling the student who is constantly at your side asking questions.

- Section 7, "Teaching Skills," presents many practical procedures that enhance teaching skills and decrease behavior problems, including "Visual Learners," a way to train students to find information on their own, and "Skills for Constructive Criticism," eight tips for motivating students to do their best work.

- Section 8, "Great 'Little Gems,'" covers a variety of topics such as "Token Economies," a point system to reward acceptable behavior, and "Sponge Activities," "filler" activities that take 5 to 15 minutes to maximize the learning time for each student.

- Section 9, "Survival Skills," gives you ideas for conserving your energy and relieving stress, such as "The 24-Hour Rule," by which you delay action for one day to let everyone cool down and better assess the situation and the options, and "Breaking Up a Fight," a suggested eight-step plan of action.

- Section 10, "Forms," provides a number of ready-to-use forms, such as the "Discipline Action Ticket," a form to be completed by the student who has broken an important rule, and five different "Student–Teacher–Parent Action Contracts" (interventions) for modifying student–teacher behavior and promoting academic growth.

Many of the topics and tools featured in this resource are advanced and strengthened by support ideas. These ideas provide very practical, easy-to-learn approaches to the management challenges that teachers face on a daily basis. You'll also find quotations that reinforce the book's underlying philosophy sprinkled throughout all sections. Many of these sayings make excellent classroom posters.

I hope you'll find that the tested, ready-to-use techniques and strategies in *One-Minute Discipline* will promote your effectiveness and help to create a positive, healthy climate for learning.

*Arnie Bianco*

# Contents

For the teacher:

"I am who I am,
and
I love what I do.
I am a teacher."

ANONYMOUS

# Philosophy

This section of <u>One-Minute Discipline</u> provides a philosophical framework for the book's techniques, strategies, and ideas. You will acquire coping skills in which to successfully complete the school year. Information is shared that enables both new and veteran teachers to chart their professional growth and progress.

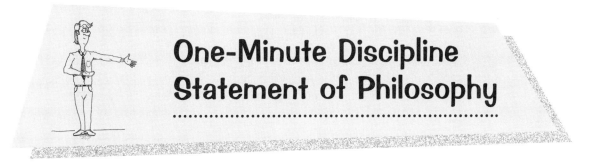

# One-Minute Discipline
# Statement of Philosophy

The following ten statements constitute the philosophical base of the *One-Minute Discipline* program. The book's techniques, ideas, and behavioral management skills have well-founded reasons for being. They are meant to enhance teacher effectiveness and promote a healthy climate for learning.

1. **Avoid sins of omission.**
   *Anytime you think the problem is "out there," THAT is the problem.* Good teachers never give up on a student. Kids come from a variety of situations and backgrounds. They often bring to the classroom different values, abilities, and personalities. When you fail to attempt to make behavioral progress with a student because of his or her parents, society, TV, or any perceived problem that is considered "out there," you commit a sin of omission. You must continue to attempt interventions that reach and improve the world of *every* student.

2. **Accept your students unconditionally.**
   *Parents make 'em and we teach 'em.* Many teachers look at their students with the following construct:

   > I am the authority.
   > They will be accountable to me.
   > I will then affirm them.
   > And I will then accept them.

   In actuality, the construct should be reversed:

   > I accept my students unconditionally (regardless of their backgrounds, life situations, abilities).
   > I will be accountable to them by being the best possible teacher I can be.
   > I will affirm our positive relationship and be committed to student growth and development.
   > I will accept and celebrate my ability to make a difference in their lives.

3. **Commit to student growth through interventions.**
   *Baby steps or small victories count!* Student progress isn't always characterized by dramatic results. It may take the form of small victories. Effective teachers record dates and anecdotal information on student growth. This notation of progress should be periodically reviewed and celebrated with the student and the parents, and should become a self-reward for you.

4. **Delegate, work smart, and save energy. It's a marathon!**
   *NEVER do ANYTHING you can delegate to a student.* The school year isn't a 50-yard dash, it's a marathon. Tasks from correcting papers to housekeeping chores should be assigned to students and aides. The secret here is for you to keep your 25 helpers as

productive as possible. Good delegation requires that you spend time in training students or aides in the proper procedures for accomplishing each task. Delegation saves valuable energy on a daily basis throughout the school year and over the course of your career.

5. **Open the gate of change.**

   *If a teacher only does what she's always done, she'll only get what she's always got.* Old habits and paradigms are very difficult to break. Teachers who continually seek improvement in classroom-management skills and in improvement of instruction stay vital and invigorated. They are excited about teaching and working with kids, and that enthusiasm "contaminates" their students. Teaching is definitely a journey and not a destination.

6. **Add more "tools" to your repertoire.**

   *When you're ripe, you rot; and when you're green, you grow.* Teaching is a profession that one never totally masters. The secret to rich, rewarding, and fruitful teaching is to continually add new instructional and behavioral strategies to your overall teaching skills. This can be accomplished by updating skills; attending workshops and conferences; visiting other classrooms; team teaching; and teaching another subject, grade level, or in another school or district.

7. **Be prevention-centered.**

   *Spend a little time now, or a whole lot of time later.* It is tantamount to your success to take time at the beginning of the school year to: establish classroom standards; delegate and TRAIN aides, and your student helpers;  create a positive rapport with parents; connect life skills with curriculum pursuits; communicate standards and curriculum information to parents; and meet with kids on a regular basis to discuss, monitor, and adjust the "state of the classroom."

8. **Promote self-reliance through transformations.**

   *Give a student a fish and you feed him for a day. Teach her to fish and you feed her for a lifetime.* Self-reliance is one of the most valuable gifts that you can give to your students. You routinely average around 500 management decisions a day. The trick here is to decrease these "transactions" and "transform" dependent students into independent and self-reliant learners.

9. **Develop relationships and a culture of appreciation.**

   *I don't care how much you know until I know how much you care.* Promote learning through a positive, supporting classroom climate. Enhance your classroom-management skills by "knowing your clients." Successful classrooms are structured, well organized, and create a warm, accepting student-centered environment. The classroom is a fun place for students and a place for everyone involved in their education to celebrate their academic and social progress.

10. **Continually improve your instructional competence.**

    *How many crayons in your crayon box?* If your crayon box is limited to the eight-pack, teaching becomes stale and a chore. Teachers who stay current, constantly update their curriculum, and search and discover new ways of doing things generate motivation and excitement about learning. This enthusiasm minimizes discipline problems because these teachers have vibrant, exciting classrooms and a 64-crayon box (with the sharpener in the back).

# One-Minute Discipline Philosophy Summary

1. Avoid sins of omission: Anytime you think the problem is "out there," THAT is the problem.

2. Accept your students unconditionally.

3. Commit to student growth through interventions. Small victories count!

4. Delegate, work smart, and save energy. It's a marathon!

5. Open the gate of change.

6. Add more "tools" to your repertoire.

7. Be prevention-centered.

8. Promote self-reliance through transformations.

9. Develop relationships and a culture of appreciation.

10. Continually improve your instructional competence.

Experience is a hard teacher because she gives the test first, the lesson afterwards.

VERNON SANDERS LAWS

**It's a Marathon!**

The school year is not a 50-yard dash . . . it's a marathon. Small amounts of valuable energy can be conserved and accumulated on a daily basis. This saved energy will better sustain you throughout the year and your career.

## How to Successfully Complete the Marathon

1. Delegate! Delegate! Delegate! NEVER do anything you can delegate to a student or aide. Why are you doing it when you have all those assistants at your fingertips?

2. Document any and all "significant" contacts you have with parents, your principal, or outside specialists. This could potentially avoid future troublesome problems.

3. Take care of yourself physically and emotionally. Exercise on a regular basis and go easy on that junk food that other teachers bring to the teachers' lounge.

4. Establish expectations at the beginning of the year and review them on a regular basis. (See Taking-Back Rule, Topic 94.)

5. Team up with another teacher(s) to team-teach, or to work on a special unit or project. This is a great idea for renewing your instructional creative juices and for having a fun time with your colleagues.

6. Cooperatively plan a future vacation. It's an excellent idea to visualize (see yourself there) your "payoff" during the marathon.

7. Have a regular "date night" with your significant other, spouse, parent, and/or kids. Keep your life balanced and never "let the sound of your own wheels drive you crazy." In short, have some fun!

8. Plan to teach at another grade level, school, or district. Don't stay in a position or place where you are unhappy.

9. Examine some of your negative habits (diet and exercise) and gradually make changes.

10. Get out of your nest and visit other teachers in your school or district or another district. There are terrific ideas out there that are just waiting for you.

11. Review and incorporate ideas from the *One-Minute Discipline* book on a regular basis.

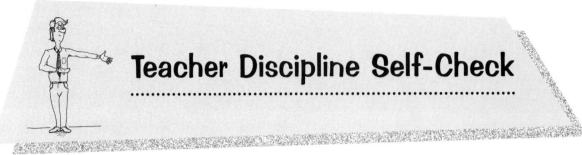

# Teacher Discipline Self-Check

The list below is designed to assist you in a self-examination of your mental health status. Are you exhibiting signs of burnout?

| Do I Need Help? | NO | | | | YES |
|---|---|---|---|---|---|
| 1. I am constantly dealing with discipline problems. | 1 | 2 | 3 | 4 | 5 |
| 2. I am making little or no progress with this class. | 1 | 2 | 3 | 4 | 5 |
| 3. It's them against me. | 1 | 2 | 3 | 4 | 5 |
| 4. I feel like this is a lost cause. | 1 | 2 | 3 | 4 | 5 |
| 5. At this age, these kids are just this way. | 1 | 2 | 3 | 4 | 5 |
| 6. With parents like these, what do you expect? | 1 | 2 | 3 | 4 | 5 |
| 7. It's TV, radio, and the movies! | 1 | 2 | 3 | 4 | 5 |
| 8. I am constantly dealing with discipline problems. | 1 | 2 | 3 | 4 | 5 |
| 9. I'm totally exhausted at the end of the day/week. | 1 | 2 | 3 | 4 | 5 |
| 10. If I only had a different principal. | 1 | 2 | 3 | 4 | 5 |

| *Scoring*: | **10 to 20** | Excellent! Help a new teacher. | **31 to 40** | Danger zone. Seek help (below). |
|---|---|---|---|---|
| | **21 to 30** | Very good. Hang in there! | **41 to 50** | Major danger! Do all of the below. |

## Help is here!

1. Seek assistance from your principal and supervisor. If comfortable, share the above results.
2. Find a mentor to discuss some of your problems and frustrations.
3. Get out of your nest and attend a conference, workshop, or convention. Get new ideas and new energy from teachers like you.
4. Team-teach with other teachers at your level or in your school. This often generates new energy for you and the team. Plan a new unit or new activity, exchange kids, cooperate on a common project.
5. Take a year off. Visit other teachers and schools throughout the year.
6. Have your mentor observe in your classroom, discuss the observation, and make suggestions.
7. Change grade levels and get reborn.
8. Have a district (central office) specialist visit you and observe in your classroom.
9. Subscribe to and read on a regular basis periodicals suitable for your grade level or subject area. Keep an open mind and be committed to trying new ideas.
10. Take care of your physical and mental health. Exercise, plan a future vacation, take a minimum of school work home, and have no school talk (or thought) after 6:00 P.M.
11. Change schools or districts.
12. Write or revise your mission statement. Why did you go into teaching? Walk your talk!

## This One's for You!

Are you taking care of yourself? Extend your career and the quality of your life by doing the following:

### Physically

- "Whenever the urge to exercise comes over me, I lie down until it passes." Exercise! This is the most important thing you can do for your present well-being and future good health.
- Find a classroom exercise activity to assist in stress reduction for your students and you.
- Proper nutrition will take care of your body so that your body will take care of you.

### Mentally

- Do recreational reading to relax and forget the day's stresses.
- Make plans for a future project, goal, or dream.
- Schedule private time to renew, strengthen, and recommit.
- Make plans for an upcoming vacation.
- Take a mini-break (vacation or short trip) away from home.

### Socially

- Plan a teaching activity with a close school friend.
- Meet socially with your friend(s) on a regular basis.
- Spend "face" time with your loved ones and family.
- Give something back. Volunteer your time, treasure, or talent to a worthy community cause.

### Spiritually

- Spend time in daily meditation or prayer.
- Attend services.
- Spend your private time in a nature place that "resonates" in you.
- Take stock of your positive progress and accomplishments and share them with someone else.

You can pay
people to teach,
but not to care.

MARVA COLLINS

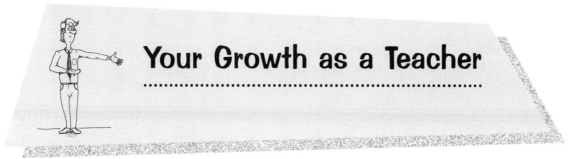

# Your Growth as a Teacher

Beginning teachers are often concerned about their professional growth and development. One in four teachers leave the profession during the first five years; in some states, the number is even higher. Novice teachers need to know "how they are doing." Match your present "situation" with the stages of development below. Remember, a teacher is a work in progress, and professional comfort, ability, and satisfaction will increase with time and experience.

### Novice

- survival
- many ups and downs (roller-coaster emotions)
- textbook bound (reliance on the teacher's edition)
- very busy and feels "alone" at times
- learns an enormous amount
- planning important and time consuming
- discipline and parent challenges

### Advanced Beginner

- episodic knowledge increases (more experiences to draw on makes decision-making easier)
- grouping knowledge increases
- sees similarities and connections
- more "strategic" at getting things done
- greater understanding as to how this lesson/unit fits into the total picture

### Competent

- feels much stronger
- discriminates curriculum decisions
- routine becomes automatic
- takes responsibility
- classroom becomes your milieu

### Master

- a sense of the situation (knows what's going on)
- decisions based on lots of experience
- higher level thinking skills and questions
- excellent assessment skills
- effortless and fluid (classroom runs like a precision watch)
- "teaching fits the vision"

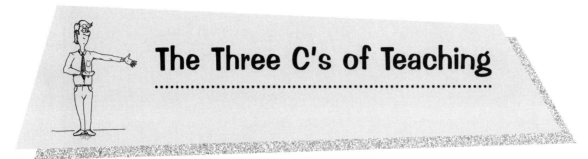

# The Three C's of Teaching

"I *care* about you as a learner and a person."

"I am *competent*. I know my stuff and I am constantly updating my subject matter ability."

"I am *committed* to improving my teaching skills, staying current and learning from my students on a daily basis."

3

Caring
Competence
Commitment

# Accepting Your Students

Some teachers approach students in the following fashion:

I am the **Authority**.

I will hold you **Accountable**.

You will then be **Affirmed**,

And eventually **Accepted**.

**Actually, the order should be reversed:**

**Acceptance**   I accept you unconditionally. Your background, parents, life style, skills, and habits are all real, but do not infringe on my total commitment to you.

**Accountable**   As your teacher, I am accountable for this year's academic, social, and emotional growth.

**Affirmation**   I see you as a work in progress and I will make a considerable contribution to your future success.

**Authority**   I will use my authority to be your advocate and be viewed as a valuable person in your life.

# Teacher Mission Statements

A teacher mission statement should be an integral part of any classroom. It states, for all to see, your philosophy, values, and goals. A laminated copy should be:

1. posted on the wall (like many successful businesses do) for all to see.

2. reviewed with students the first week of school.

3. referred to with students during the school year.

4. referred to by the teacher as a tool for routine self-examination and renewal.

The following is an anonymous sample by a new teacher.

---

## My Mission Statement

- To empower.

- To impart self-esteem.

- To be a positive role model.

- To be at least one person in each student's universe who unconditionally believes in his/her ability to "be all that (he/she) can be" . . . either in my classroom or anywhere else.

- To provide a classroom atmosphere in which there is freedom and safety to make mistakes and take risks. Not being perfect the first time out is part of learning, growing, and becoming educated.

- To accept and respect each student in all his/her unique individuality and to communicate that acceptance and respect to the student.

- To impart skills; the "proper" use of the English language; and fluent, coherent, and correct writing.

- To open the world of literature to students.

---

If there is
no yellow brick
road and no
Emerald City,
nothing will
happen.

MIKE VANCE

# Exercise! Exercise! Exercise!

America appears to be headed toward a national crisis as it faces the challenge of more and more overweight and even obese children. Some experts describe the dilemma as one of epidemic proportions that will lead to a significant increase in diabetes, asthma, and heart disease. To complicate the situation, districts that face budget problems often curtail or eliminate their physical education programs.

## How can the classroom teacher help?

1. Whenever possible, do not use recess as a time to ground young perpetrators. THEY NEED EXERCISE THE MOST!

2. Schedule your own P.E. sessions. Delegate all routine matters (getting and returning equipment, etc.) to your kids.

3. Acquire—and use—a book of indoor classroom physical education activities. (Check your local teaching tools store.)

4. Buy a movement/dance tape to use when your teacher "withitness" tells you that a change of activity is needed in order to get some oxygen to the brains of your students.

**Suggested tape available at Borders or Barnes and Noble:**

Sesame Street's *Hot! Hot! Hot! Dance Songs,* including:

"The Lambada"
"Clucky Clucky Chicken"
"Doing the Penguin"

# Know Your "Clients"

Kids are our clients. As in the business world, it pays to know the needs of your clients. This section provides an opportunity for you to get to know students' backgrounds, home information, likes and dislikes, and feelings about this school year and past years' experiences. It includes several surveys, reports, and support ideas that will give you objective and useful information for meeting the social, academic, and behavioral needs of your students.

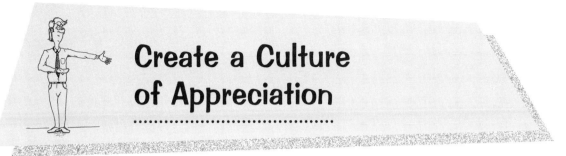

# Create a Culture of Appreciation

A teacher is a social architect who creates a culture of appreciation in the classroom. The phrase *social architecture* is significant because it implies that a "culture" is created by the teacher and the residents of that classroom.

One can see the "structure" when you enter a classroom. It is continually changing and evolving and must be guided in the right direction. The teacher is the point person for that journey. The teacher is caring, committed, and competent, whose mission is to be there for these learners. The teacher cares about the students' academic growth and their growth as social citizens. The teacher's competence is clear. He knows his stuff. He has "mastered" his subject matter and his greatest joy is to share that information with students on a daily basis.

The teacher lives for the sweet moments when the light bulb comes on in the minds of these students. All is right in this room, and the teacher and class celebrate their group progress and individual victories. The teacher is most pleased with this creation.

We make a living
by what we get,
but we make a life
by what we give.

WINSTON CHURCHILL

## Help Create a Terrific School Community

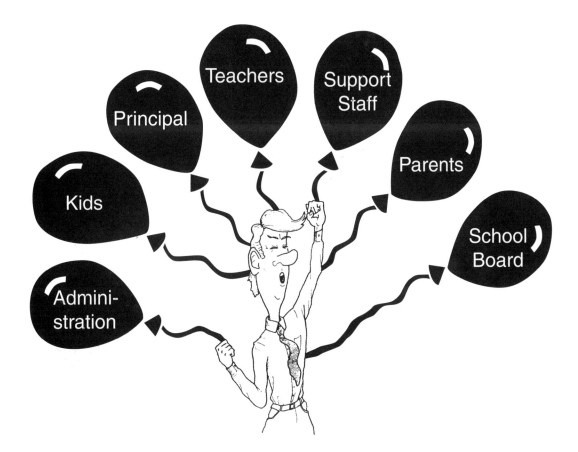

A terrific school community is one in which each segment of the community feels that it:

1. is an important part of the school system.

2. has a stake in the overall plan or mission.

3. is a legitimate card-carrying member (it belongs).

4. has a certain degree of "power" in the organization.

5. is recognized as an integral player on the team.

# Icebreaker One:
# The Student Shield

**What?** An icebreaker is used the first week of school in an attempt to get to know each individual student.

**Why?** It is very important for you to know as much as possible about each student early in the year. This personalized approach promotes motivation for learning and a positive relationship between you and students.

**How?** Have a coat of arms completed by each student, which can then be displayed on bulletin boards and eventually placed in each student information folder.

Some examples include:

- Pets
- Family
- Things I like to do
- Sports
- Leisure activities
- Movies

- Foods
- Video games
- Careers
- Happy times or happy places
- Friends

- Vacations
- Books
- Dreams and nightmares
- Hopes and dreams
- Hobbies

# Icebreaker Two:
# Backpack Introductions

**What?** This icebreaker, scheduled for near the beginning of the school year, is a fun way to obtain information about each student.

**Why?** This activity promotes student–teacher and student–student relationships early in the school year. Student–teacher rapport is enhanced by "getting to know" each student on a personal basis.

**How?** Begin the activity by bringing "your life" to school in a backpack. Personal items representing your life are removed from the pack and shared with the class. These items may include photos, awards, trophies, CDs, clothing, ticket stubs, musical instruments, valued object memorabilia, and much more. Each student follows the procedure throughout the beginning weeks of school.

**"I don't care how much you know until I know how much you care."**

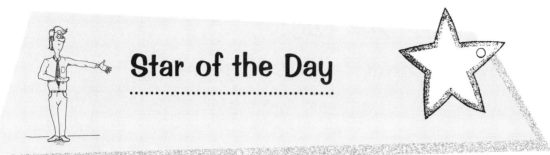

# Star of the Day

"Star of the Day" (every star must have his or her day) is a fun way to pick the student of the day (or week). Using your criteria, you select the honoree and the chosen student receives special privileges for the day.

Privileges may include such things as:

- special messenger duty.
- a seat of honor for the day/week. (Some teachers bring in a special desk or upholstered chair for the seat of honor.)
- snack and drink privileges.
- lunch in the room.
- first in line to special classes or lunch.

(For more, use your imagination and/or ask the kids.)

# Icebreaker Three:
# Student Survey

| **What?** | The student survey, the third icebreaker, is used to obtain information concerning students' past experiences in school. |
|---|---|
| **Why?** | After you survey a total class(es), you have some valuable information as to the qualities of past teachers who "connect" with kids. The survey is not meant as a personality contest, but an opportunity to discover what "works" with school children. |
| **How?** | Use the survey provided. Surveys should be anonymous and results may be shared with the class at your discretion. |

# Student Survey

> *Rules for completion:* 1. Do not use names of past teachers.
> 2. Be specific and honest in your responses.

1. What school event will you remember for many years to come? What happened that you can remember so clearly?

   _____

   _____

   _____

2. List the special qualities of your BEST teacher.

   _____

   _____

   _____

3. List the special qualities of your FAVORITE teacher.

   _____

   _____

   _____

4. You wake up tomorrow morning and YOU are a teacher in another school. What good ideas from THIS school would you bring to your new school?

   _____

   _____

   _____

# Student Input Class Survey

The Student Input Class Survey is an excellent way for you to enhance your relationship with the class. This simple survey provides you with some important feedback from your pupils. You can also complete the survey (orally) on/with the class or with individual students. The results of the survey are used to improve relationships and to prevent problems before they get more serious. The survey should be given periodically throughout the year.

The results of the survey enable you to:

1. Head off a potential problem(s).

2. Reinforce positive aspects of student–teacher interactions (warm strokes for the teacher).

3. Share positive results with your principal.

4. Promote the classroom philosophy of developing a culture of appreciation.

# Student Input Class Survey

Remember, no names!

1. What are the things you enjoy most about this school year?

   _____

   _____

   _____

   _____

   _____

   _____

2. What are the things you would like the teacher to stop doing?

   _____

   _____

   _____

   _____

   _____

   _____

3. What new things would you like to see happen in this class?

   _____

   _____

   _____

   _____

   _____

   _____

# Classroom Atmosphere Survey

**What?**  The *classroom atmosphere survey* objectively measures the feelings of students toward you and the established climate of a classroom.

**Why?**  Positive student–teacher relationships promote learning in the classroom. This survey gives you baseline data as to the classroom "climate" you have established in your class. The survey positively reinforces you and provides information important to improving relationships.

**How?**  Give the survey after about six weeks of the school year. Make adjustments (as needed) and then retest after another six weeks. Survey results may be shared with the principal or supervisor.

# Classroom Atmosphere Survey

*Directions:* Please complete this survey by circling "No," "Sometimes," or "Yes" for each question.

| | | | |
|---|---|---|---|
| 1. This classroom is very enjoyable. | No | Sometimes | Yes |
| 2. I complete my work every day. | No | Sometimes | Yes |
| 3. My teacher knows about my family. | No | Sometimes | Yes |
| 4. My teacher really knows the subject(s). | No | Sometimes | Yes |
| 5. My teacher is good at handling problems. | No | Sometimes | Yes |
| 6. I dislike school. | No | Sometimes | Yes |
| 7. Kids in this class are always willing to share. | No | Sometimes | Yes |
| 8. I tell my parents about things I do in school. | No | Sometimes | Yes |
| 9. Talking and sharing ideas are important here. | No | Sometimes | Yes |
| 10. I have good friends in this class. | No | Sometimes | Yes |
| 11. I am an important part of this classroom. | No | Sometimes | Yes |
| 12. People in this school really enjoy kids. | No | Sometimes | Yes |
| 13. I wish I have another teacher like this one next year. | No | Sometimes | Yes |

14. I can get help from my teacher.                         **No**    **Sometimes**    **Yes**

15. I feel good when I talk to my teacher.                   **No**    **Sometimes**    **Yes**

16. My teacher is good at handling discipline problems.      **No**    **Sometimes**    **Yes**

17. My teacher is usually too busy to help me.               **No**    **Sometimes**    **Yes**

18. There always seems to be interesting things to do        **No**    **Sometimes**    **Yes**
    in this class.

19. If I don't understand, I can always find help            **No**    **Sometimes**    **Yes**
    in this room.

20. My teacher is a great storyteller.                       **No**    **Sometimes**    **Yes**

21. My teacher encourages me to have new and                 **No**    **Sometimes**    **Yes**
    different ideas.

22. I am a proud member of this class.                       **No**    **Sometimes**    **Yes**

23. My teacher tells us what she or he does                  **No**    **Sometimes**    **Yes**
    on weekends.

24. Our classroom rules are easy to understand               **No**    **Sometimes**    **Yes**
    and follow.

25. We are frequently reminded of our class rules.           **No**    **Sometimes**    **Yes**

A little nonsense
now and then
is relished by the
wisest men.

ROALD DAHL

# Reinforcer Survey

| | |
|---|---|
| **What?** | The *reinforcer survey* identifies students' areas of interest and what they like to do, and provides general background information. |
| **Why?** | The results of the survey enable you to reward students for acceptable behavior and work accomplished based on their interests and things they like to do. It also creates a positive tone in the classroom. |
| **How?** | Use the survey provided. |

# Reinforcer Survey

Name _____     Date _____

1.  After school I like to _____
    _____.

2.  My favorite TV program is _____
    _____.

3.  My favorite activity at school is _____
    _____.

4.  My best friend is _____
    _____.

5.  My favorite CD is _____
    _____.

6.  My favorite subject at school is _____
    _____.

7.  I like to read books about _____
    _____.

8.  My hobbies are _____
    _____.

9.  My favorite pet (animal) is _____
    _____.

10. Three things I like to do most are _____
    _____.

# Reinforcer Rules

1. Reinforcers should be low in cost.
2. Reinforcers should require a relatively small amount of your time.
3. Reinforcers should be simple and, in most cases, unsophisticated.

The teacher supplies:

- immediate feedback to students
- a variety of reinforcers to maintain student interest
- excitement and enthusiasm for the reinforcee and the activity
- the exact reason why the student is receiving the reinforcer
- frequent positive verbal and visual reinforcement
- the class survey that identifies student ideas for reinforcers

# Citizenship Program Report

**What?**   The *citizenship program report* defines the total school program for students and parents.

**Why?**   This proactive plan articulates the school program at the beginning of the school year. It is an excellent tool for upper elementary or middle school students. Keeping these adolescent citizens as busy as possible builds school spirit and focuses attention on positive contributions to school and pupil development.

**How?**   Make all students aware of the citizenship program the first week of school. You, the principal, or school counselor meet with each student at the end of each quarter to award points. You, the student, and parent sign-off on the form provided. At the end of the year, awards for most points can be given in each area and for grand totals *(optional)*. Criteria areas are easily adapted to each individual classroom or school program.

# Citizenship Program Report

Name _____     Date _____

Teacher _____

| Curriculum | | | | | Co-Curriculum | | | | | School Service & Leadership | | | | |
|---|---|---|---|---|---|---|---|---|---|---|---|---|---|---|
| 1st | 2nd | 3rd | 4th | | 1st | 2nd | 3rd | 4th | | 1st | 2nd | 3rd | 4th | |
| — | — | — | — | effort | — | — | — | — | D.A.R.E | — | — | — | — | student council |
| — | — | — | — | grade improvement | — | — | — | — | Project Pride | — | — | — | — | yearbook |
| — | — | — | — | spelling bee | — | — | — | — | camp | — | — | — | — | tutor |
| — | — | — | — | science fair | — | — | — | — | band | — | — | — | — | class citizenship |
| — | — | — | — | love of reading | — | — | — | — | skating party | — | — | — | — | cabin leader |
| — | — | — | — | geography bee | — | — | — | — | bingo fundraiser | — | — | — | — | office aide |
| — | — | — | — | quiz bowl | — | — | — | — | carnival helper | — | — | — | — | library aide |
| — | — | — | — | spell-a-thon | — | — | — | — | other | — | — | — | — | candy fundraiser |
| — | — | — | — | stock market game | — | — | — | — | | — | — | — | — | discipline tickets |
| — | — | — | — | homework record | — | — | — | — | | — | — | — | — | attendance |
| — | — | — | — | other | — | — | — | — | | — | — | — | — | dance committee |
| — | — | — | — | | — | — | — | — | | — | — | — | — | other |

| Curriculum | Co-Curriculum | School Service & Leadership |
|---|---|---|
| Total _____ | Total _____ | Total _____ |

## Signatures

| Parent(s) | Teacher | Student |
|---|---|---|
| 1. _____ | 1. _____ | 1. _____ |
| 2. _____ | 2. _____ | 2. _____ |
| 3. _____ | 3. _____ | 3. _____ |
| 4. _____ | 4. _____ | 4. _____ |

Real education
consists of
drawing the best
out of yourself.

MOHANDAS K. GANDHI

# Characteristics of a Healthy Classroom

- To empower
    - To impart skills
        - To impart self-esteem
            - To facilitate learning
                - To be a positive role model
                    - To accept and respect each student

            - To open the world to the student

| | |
|---|---|
| **What?** | A healthy classroom maintains the dignity of all students by providing an optimum environment for living and learning. |
| **Why?** | Healthy classrooms promote learning. They are motivation for both the students and you. |
| **How?** | Establish the characteristics listed by providing them as a first-week document/newsletter or by posting them as a mission statement. |

# Characteristics of a Healthy Classroom

1. Trust is established.

2. Fear is minimized.

3. The student perceives the benefits of changing his or her behavior.

4. Education is structured to help the student see different alternatives and to provide the opportunity to make choices that are real, meaningful, and significant.

5. The evaluation of learning actively engages the student.

6. Learning is perceived as meaningful.

7. True learning is genuinely pleasurable.

8. True education helps students learn a process for successful living that applies to any situation.

9. Learning includes the cognitive and affective domains. Feelings and thoughts should be incorporated for learning to have personal and lasting usefulness.

# Meeting Students' Needs

**The need to belong:**

> to feel accepted; to be a member of the group or class

**The need for power:**

> not so much power over others as power to control part of one's own life and power to do things competently

**The need for freedom:**

> to feel at least partly in control of self, self-reliant, without constant direction from others

**The need for fun:**

> for enjoyment, for pleasure, for satisfaction

**What?**   Author William Glasser* defined the four fundamental needs that play powerful roles in student behavior.

**Why?**   By identifying these needs, you can structure the classroom environment to meet the needs for most students.

**How?**   Structure the classroom to meet students' fundamental needs. This motivates students to:

1. Work as a group (need to belong) and not as an individual (traditional classroom).

2. Work on behalf of the group.

3. Help weaker students as the stronger students meet their needs for power.

4. Accept contributions to the group from weaker students.

5. Help each other and become free from overdependence on the teacher.

*William Glasser, author of *Control Theory in the Classroom*

We teachers
can only help
the work going on,
as servants wait upon
a master.

MARIA MONTESSORI

# Interest Boosting*

**What?**   *Interest boosting* is a process in which you make a special effort to show genuine interest in a student's work.

**Why?**   Students often show signs of boredom or restlessness. Interest boosting demonstrates to students that you are concerned about them as individuals and their academic growth and development.

> "I don't care how much you know (or who you are) until I know how much you care."

**How?**   Look at the student's work, compliment his or her effort, and make suggestions as needed.

> "The matter is that you matter.
> Beyond this there is no need.
> Because if you matter, then all else matters."

*Term by Jacob Kounin, author of *Discipline and Group Management in Classrooms*

43

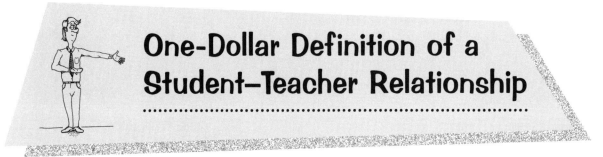

# One-Dollar Definition of a Student-Teacher Relationship

It's a relationship and, like any other relationship, it requires attention and nurturing. If you find that you are frustrated and not succeeding with a youngster, you might want to use the one-dollar definition of a relationship to evaluate what is really happening. If things aren't going well, it could be that bad times are dominating your interactions. Review your "contacts" with the student for about a week and be objective in evaluating what is happening. Are bad times outweighing the good ones? Strive to create as many good times as possible between you and your students.

Good
Times
minus
Bad
Times

# Journal Writing

Journal writing is an excellent way of enhancing teacher–student communication while providing a relevant and meaningful writing experience.

One method is to have the kids write (every day) in a journal notebook and then share (exclusively and confidentially) the entry with you on a daily basis. The idea below is an easy variation on the journal-writing idea. You:

1. Explain the "How Do You Feel Today?" form (provided). (These are placed in individual notebooks after you have read and initialed them.)

2. Provide a notebook of forms to use upon entering class.

3. Explain that you may (may not) give direct feedback on each form every day.

4. Schedule, if needed or requested, a longer "chat" with students.

# How Do You Feel Today?

Name _____    Date _____

Teacher's initials _____

Circle the learner (below) who represents the way you feel today. Write a short paragraph about WHY you feel that way.

_____
_____
_____
_____
_____
_____
_____
_____
_____

I would like to talk about this with my teacher.    YES    NO

# Age of Squirreliness

## Physical Characteristics

1. Average weight gain of 10 pounds.
2. Average height growth of two inches.
3. Sexual maturation and growth.
4. Concern with appearance reflecting peer and current fads.
5. Alternating periods of hyperactivity and fatigue.
6. Digestive system overburdened with large quantities of poorly selected foods.

## Social Characteristics

1. Diminishing parent allegiances and stronger peer allegiances.
2. Attempts to gain social acceptance of peers.
3. Vacillation between desire for direction and the demand for independence.
4. Willingness to work hard if social rewards are involved.

## Emotional Characteristics

1. Confusing responses mask anxiety and fear with reassuring bravado; shyness with noisiness.
2. Tendency to make exaggerated responses to anything with sexual implications.
3. Desire for attention, without regard for how it is secured.
4. Ignorance of expressed or implied criticism from adult sources.
5. Ignorance, ridicule, and defiance of adult convention.

## Intellectual Characteristics

1. Pressure, often excessive, to succeed academically.
2. Heightened egocentrism.
3. Wide range of skills, interests, and abilities.
4. Increased concern with intellectual, sociological, moral, and ethical issues.

**What?** The *age of squirreliness* describes the unique characteristics of middle school/junior high young people.

**Why?** Understanding that early adolescents can be "squirrels" assists you in "knowing" your students and the dramatic changes that are occurring with them. It also helps you maintain your sanity knowing that this is "normal" behavior for young teens.

**How?** Realize that these kids are unique. Good teachers who find these grade levels a great place to be really add enjoyment to their teaching . . . they have found their milieu.

Children today
are tyrants.
They contradict
their parents,
gobble their food,
and tyrannize their
teachers.

SOCRATES (470–399 B.C.)

# Dignity for All

**What?** You must remember that you are the adult and that a student should never be put in a psychological corner.

**Why?** One of your main missions is to develop positive relationships with students. Learning is enhanced when students feel comfortable in class and like their teacher.

**How?** Catch kids being good. You should *not* use the following phrases: "What are you doing?" "Why are you doing that?" "Don't you know any better?"

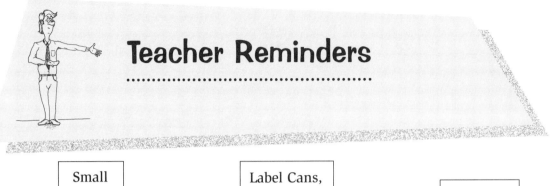

# Teacher Reminders

# Only the Brave Should Teach

Only the brave.

Only the brave should teach.

Only those who love the young should teach.

Teaching is a vocation.

It is as sacred as the priesthood; as innate
   a desire as inescapable as the genius which
   compels an artist.

If he has not the concern for humanity,
   the love of living creatures, the vision
   of the priest and the artist, he must
   not teach.

PEARL S. BUCK

# Life Skills

| **What?** | *Life skills* is the system on which a class or school operates. |
|---|---|
| **Why?** | Kids bring a number of social systems to the schoolhouse door. Some are excellent while others are totally lacking. Life skills act as a model for training and reinforcing acceptable standards and principles of behavior. |
| **How?** | Highlight the life skills listed throughout the school year. For example: "Class, this week's life skill is respect. What is respect? What would it look like if you saw it? Who is brave enough to give me a recent example of a situation where you used or saw respect?" (Laminate the list, post it in your classroom, and send copies home to parents.) |

"Life Skill of the Week" should be repeated the second semester of the school year.

# List of Life Skills

**Respect:** Value the worth of another person.

**Integrity:** Do the right thing.

**Initiative:** Do something because it needs to be done.

**Flexibility:** Be able to change plans when necessary.

**Perseverance:** Keep trying, no matter what.

**Organization:** Plan ahead to keep things in order.

**Sense of Humor:** Laugh and be playful without hurting others.

**Effort:** Try your hardest.

**Common Sense:** Use good judgment.

**Problem-solving:** Solve problems, even when it is very difficult.

**Responsibility:** Do what you are supposed to do, when you are supposed to do it.

**Patience:** Wait calmly for someone or something.

**Friendship:** Make and keep a friend, so that you care for and trust each other.

**Curiosity:** Want to learn or know about one's world.

**Cooperation:** Work together toward a common goal or purpose.

**Caring:** Feel concern for others.

**Courage:** Act according to one's beliefs.

# Principles for Tomorrow

## Citizenship

- Respect for United States Constitution
- Awareness of international relationships
- Justice and fairness
- Patriotism
- Property rights
- Due process of law
- Freedom of thought and action
- Respect for the law

## Care of the Environment

- Respect for land, air, and water
- Care for all living beings

## Respect for Others

- Courtesy
- Cooperativeness
- Honesty
- Loyalty
- Moderation
- Understanding of various ethnic traditions
- Human worth and dignity
- Tolerance

## Respect for Self

- Accountability
- Courage
- Thrift
- Self-esteem and pride
- Self-discipline
- Self-reliance
- Cleanliness
- Personal responsibilities for one's actions

## Respect for Knowledge

- Desire to learn
- Creative thinking
- Application of knowledge
- Objectivity
- Order

# What Is Success?

To laugh often and much;

To win the respect of intelligent people

And the affection of children;

To appreciate beauty;

To find the best in others;

To leave the world a bit better,

    whether by a healthy child,

    a garden patch

    or a redeemed social condition;

To know even one life has breathed

    easier because you have lived;

This is to have succeeded.

RALPH WALDO EMERSON

# Class Meetings*

**What?**  *Class meetings* are a forum where students discuss any group problem.

**Why?**  Without group assistance, students tend to evade problems, depend on others to solve their problems, or withdraw.

**How?**  Follow these guidelines for meetings:

1. Any group member problem may be discussed; a problem may be introduced by a student or you.
2. The discussion should be directed toward solving the problem.
3. The discussion atmosphere should be nonjudgmental and nonpunitive.
4. The solution should not include punishment or fault finding.
5. The meeting should be conducted with you and the students seated in a tight circle.
6. Meetings should be held often and not exceed 30 to 45 minutes, depending on the age of the students.

*Term by William Glasser, author of *Control Theory in the Classroom*

# Home and School

Parents are also our clients. They are the other half of the important home–school partnership. This section includes ideas for promoting positive home–school communication and specific examples of ways to keep your parent-partners informed. Skills for parent conferences and dealing with upset parents are also included.

# Newsletters

·······························

**What?** Newsletters are a form of home–school communication designed to inform parents about programs, expectations, and student progress.

**Why?** Research indicates that teachers who make a concerted effort to inform parents are held in higher esteem and receive more support from the public.

**How?** *Part 1.* Send home a first-edition newsletter the first week of school outlining for parents classroom policies in regard to: conduct, materials, absences, make-up work, late work, tardies, passes, homework, dress code, materials, extra credit, grades, etc. Parents save the newsletter but return a signed form that they have read the information.

*Part 2.* Send home a monthly (or more frequent) newsletter to parents dealing with such topics as: the curriculum, standards of conduct, academic expectations, class/student progress reports, information about upcoming activities, special assistance (aide work) needs for the class, and so on.

# Trifold Information for Students and Parents

The trifold idea is a very inexpensive way to tell students about: your background, important information concerning the new year, and a brief summary of class rules.

Here are suggested pages:

## Front of Trifold

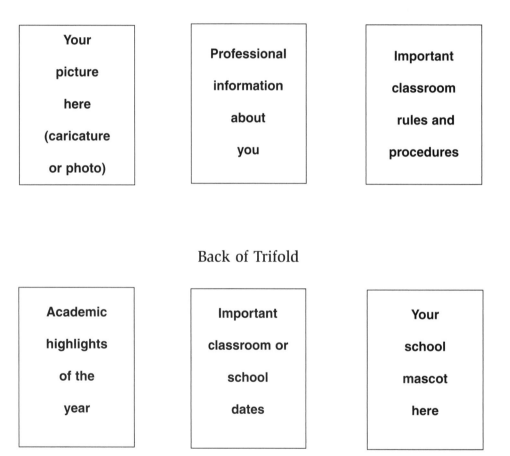

| Your picture here (caricature or photo) | Professional information about you | Important classroom rules and procedures |

## Back of Trifold

| Academic highlights of the year | Important classroom or school dates | Your school mascot here |

# School or Classroom Folders

School folders are an inexpensive way to share general school or classroom information with students and parents. They also have pocket areas for papers, homework, etc. If school folders are not available, the same idea can be used by an individual classroom teacher. The inside and back of the folder may contain information on:

- Attendance
- Tardiness
- Lockers
- Library
- Grading
- Discipline
- Vandalism
- Telephone
- Insurance
- Time Schedule
- Bus Regulations

- Lost and Found
- Medication
- Dress Code
- Textbooks
- Cafeteria
- Assemblies
- Smoking Restrictions
- Guidance
- Report Cards
- Health Room
- Student Council

- Drug Policy
- Fire Drills
- Honor Roll
- Athletics

Be sure to put the school name or classroom grade on the front cover.

# School Mascots

In many schools, kids, parents, and teachers identify with a school mascot. The mascot's logo appears on everything from stationery to T-shirts. This special symbol contributes to the atmosphere of the school and promotes a positive esprit de corps (the common spirit existing in the members of a group). There are many traditional mascots to choose from (Eagles, Coyotes, Hawks, Titans, etc.), but "Bumper Bear" (below) was a unique idea created with the help of a school parent.

**Planners**

Planners help students organize and manage their time more effectively so that they stay on top of school work.

Several companies offer planners with these features:

- 3-hole punched to fit a binder
- class schedules
- full-year calendar
- achievement record page
- parent note section (home communication)
- study tips
- reminders to bring home
- how to do a long-term assignment
- telephone and e-mail directory
- school name or logo imprinted on the cover
- special dates, birthdays, events, etc.

- teaching activities
- grammar guide
- study-buddies page
- seating charts
- study strategies
- trouble words
- parts of speech
- mathematics charts
- periodic table
- world map
- time zones

Two addresses for planners are:

Quality Planners
P.O. Box 599
Jericho, NY 11753

Premier Agendas, Inc.
2000 Kentucky Street
Bellingham, WA 98226

TOPIC 15

# Parent Conferences

**What?**  Parent conferences are regular meetings to discuss pupil progress or concerns.

**Why?**  Regular meetings with parents hold all parties (student, parent, teacher) accountable for pupil growth and development.

**How?**  Follow these conference guidelines:

1. Plan (put our goals in writing).
2. Bring support materials (cumulative folders, pupil progress folder, testing, etc.).
3. Professional setting (no interruptions).
4. State purpose and have student present.
5. Use clear, easy-to-understand language. Avoid education jargon.
6. Invite specialists (reading, speech, psychologist) as needed.
7. Listen to parents' input.
8. Develop a positive plan and assign individual obligations.
9. Summarize and present a monitoring plan. (What happens next and when do we meet again to discuss progress?)
10. Refer to home–school relationship as a partnership. (**Teacher: "We're here, as partners, in the best interest of your child."**)
11. Document meeting with a letter or brief summary.

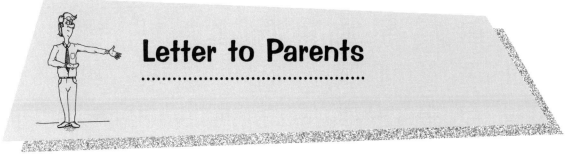

# Letter to Parents

What is the student like at home? How well do the parents know their child?

Get to know your students through the eyes of their parents by sending home the letter provided here.

# Please Tell Me About Your Child

Dear Parent(s):

We are off to a great start to our school year. I have established an individual progress folder on each student in the class. As part of that folder, I would like to add a short general information page from you. I will be sharing academic and social progress with you at our first parent–teacher conference and throughout the year.

Please include such things as your child's:

| | | |
|---|---|---|
| personal history | likes and dislikes | sports |
| friends | favorite meals | hobbies |
| vacations | favorite TV programs or movies | books |
| habits | dreams | future goals |
| fun things you do together | "career" highlights | |

Many thanks!

Teacher _____     Date _____

- - - - - - - - - - - - - - - - - - - - - - - - - - - - - - - - - - - - - - - - - - - - - - - - - - - - - - - - -

Dear Teacher:

_____

_____

_____

_____

_____

_____

_____

_____

_____

_____

_____

_____

_____

_____

Parent's name _____     Date _____

# Excellent Service for Parent Clients

## 10 Offenses Against Parents You Can Correct

1. "I don't know."
2. "I don't care."
3. "I can't be bothered."
4. "I don't like you."
5. "I know it all."
6. "You don't know anything."
7. "We don't want your kind here."
8. "Don't come back."
9. "I'm right and you're wrong."
10. "Hurry up and wait."

## Put Parents on Cloud Nine

1. RULES: Make parents feel:

   - Heard
   - Helped
   - Understood
   - Respected
   - Appreciated
   - Liked

2. Parents want:

   - Reliability (dependable and accurate reports and conferences)
   - Knowledge and courtesy
   - Empathy (caring)
   - Responsiveness

3. Fair-Fix: "Don't fight . . . I want to make it right."

   - Listen (to their story)
   - Probe (ask questions and get information)
   - Solve

# Angry Parents

Dealing with upset parents can be a real challenge. This information should be of assistance during a stressful encounter.

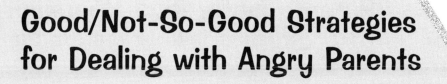

# Good/Not-So-Good Strategies for Dealing with Angry Parents

Good

Not So Good

**Good**

1. "Let me think about that."
   (Shows that you are taking the concern seriously.)

2. "I can tell you're upset. Please tell me more."
   (Message: "I want to help you.")

3. "Please speak more slowly."
   (This technique assists in getting parents to lower their voice.)

4. "I see how that would upset you."
   ("I'm sorry you feel that way.")

5. "What would you like me to do?"

6. FEEL—FELT—FOUND

   "I know exactly how you feel."

   "The same thing happened to my daughter in sixth grade."

   "I found that, if we communicate on a weekly basis, we should be able to get the situation under control."

**Not So Good**

1. "This is why the problem exists." (At this early stage, the parent isn't interested in your side of the story.)

2. "Well, it was just a matter of time." (No sarcastic counterattacking.)

3. "Please lower your voice." (Parents will not lower their voices because they feel that by complying with the request, they are weakening their position.)

4. "Well, sometimes life just isn't fair."

5. "My hands are tied."

# Parent Conference Checklist

### Preparation

- ☐ Plan. (Write outcome goals.)
- ☐ Prepare/bring pupil information folder.
- ☐ Use a professional setting.
- ☐ Accept no interruptions.
- ☐ Set strategies.
- ☐ Review cumulative folder.

### Conference

- ☐ Have student present (in most cases).
- ☐ Follow plan and do not get sidetracked.
- ☐ Invite specialists as needed.
- ☐ State purpose. ("We're here in the best interest of your child.")
- ☐ Present information using easy-to-understand language.
- ☐ Bring cumulative folder.
- ☐ Ask for parent input.
- ☐ Listen.
- ☐ Develop group plan.
- ☐ Suggest home activities.
- ☐ Have everyone state future obligations.
- ☐ Summarize plan.
- ☐ Follow-up conference in writing.
- ☐ Document all contacts.
- ☐ Present monitoring plan and date for next contact or meeting (if needed).

| | |
|---|---|
| **What?** | Parent conferences are very important in maintaining a healthy home–school partnership. |
| **Why?** | Parents and teachers working together in the best interest of the child are powerful resources in maintaining classroom behavior. The message becomes "We're all on the same team," NOT "It's us versus them." |
| **How?** | Review the checklist prior to a conference. |

## Notes Sent Home

Notes sent home provide important documentation for your contacts with parents, outside agencies, the principal, other teachers, or other professionals. The note is sent home and a copy is placed in the student's individual folder. The notes/folder can then be used at parent conferences and at meetings with the child study team or the school principal.

Document!

Document!!

Document!!!

To: _____   Date_____

_____

_____

_____

_____

_____

_____

_____

_____

_____

_____

_____

_____

_____

Teacher _____   Parent _____

Top copy: Home or outside agency      File: Bottom copy

# Help from Parent Volunteers

## Parent volunteers help at school by:

- being a classroom aide
- grading papers at home
- sharing hobbies and career information
- going on field trips
- helping with special events, such as a field day, play, party, etc.

## Your recruiting newsletter includes:

- days of week/month parents can help
- times
- parent skills (typing, clerical, correcting)

## Teacher planning:

- Prepare kids for special classroom helpers.
- Remind kids to show their appreciation for the special assistance.
- Plan for the role of the aides in your instructional program.
- Have a designated work area for the aides.
- Have an appreciation luncheon sometime during the year.

## Schedule a "training" workshop with parents at the start of the year. Include:

- Confidentiality issues
- How to use various machines
- Discussion of the aide's role in the room, on a field trip, or during a lesson
- Discussion of the nature of different tasks and which aides will "fit" which jobs

# Esprit de Corps

*Esprit de Corps* is the common spirit in the members of a group inspiring enthusiasm, and strong devotion and regard for the honor of the group.

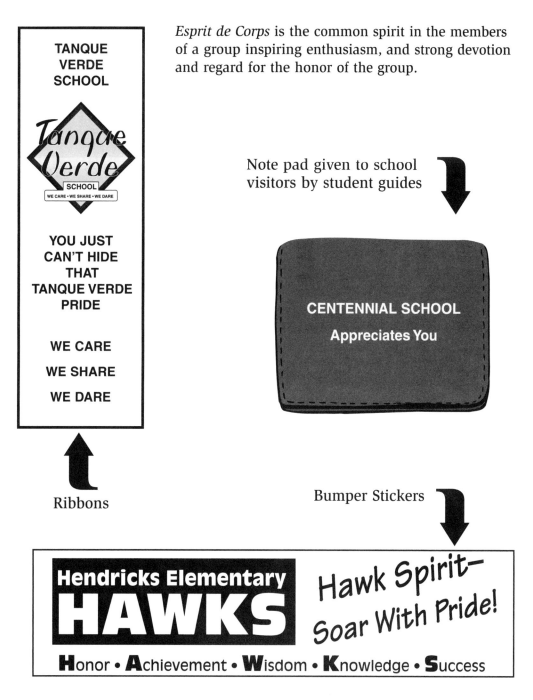

**TANQUE VERDE SCHOOL**

*Tanque Verde*
SCHOOL
WE CARE • WE SHARE • WE DARE

**YOU JUST CAN'T HIDE THAT TANQUE VERDE PRIDE**

**WE CARE**

**WE SHARE**

**WE DARE**

Ribbons

Note pad given to school visitors by student guides

**CENTENNIAL SCHOOL**

**Appreciates You**

Bumper Stickers

**Hendricks Elementary HAWKS** Hawk Spirit— Soar With Pride!

**H**onor • **A**chievement • **W**isdom • **K**nowledge • **S**uccess

# Homework

| | |
|---|---|
| **What?** | A homework policy clearly provides students and parents with information required for understanding the purpose and character of homework assignments. |
| **Why?** | A detailed homework policy facilitates communication between home and school. It also enhances student time-management skills, defines teacher expectations, and explains to parents the benefits of homework. |
| **How?** | Publish your policy the first week of school. It should include: |

1. Frequency and types of homework
2. Guidelines as to when and how work is to be completed
3. Homework and its relation to grades
4. The role of parents

The benefits of homework include:

1. Reinforces skills
2. Teaches students to work independently
3. Builds responsibility
4. Helps students with organizational and time-management skills

# SECTION 4

# The First Week of School

The beginning of school is a crucial time for you because it is the opening act for the remainder of the school year. This section contains valuable information that will assist you in establishing standards and expectations, rules, procedures, and responsibilities.

# Who Wants to Be Class Champion?

Use the 2-page reproducible and this fun game to establish or review rules, procedures, and expectations at the beginning of the year. As you review the questions, take time to *elaborate* on the meaning of the answers toward the goal of a successful school year.

Life Lines  =  1.  Ask a friend.

2.  50–50

3.  Ask the class.

The "Class Champion" ($1,000,000 winner) gets the seat of honor or a similar "reward" until a new champion is crowned. The next contest can take the form of a review for a test with the questions submitted by students and organized by you. These questions can be used with future groups.

**Answers for "Who Wants to Be Class Champion?"**

This activity is designed to introduce and reinforce class rules the first week of school. The "test" objectives are to have some fun while reviewing important behavioral expectations for the new year. Answers may vary with each class and you are encouraged to substitute your own questions as needed.

| | | | | | |
|---|---|---|---|---|---|
| $100: | d | $8,000: | a | $125,000: | d |
| $200: | b | $16,000: | d | $250,000: | d |
| $500: | b | $32,000: | b | $500,000: | a |
| $1,000: | d | $64,000: | d | $1,000,000: | c |

# Questions for "Who Wants to Be Class Champion?"

**$100 Level**

Who is/was the best teacher who ever lived?

    a. Socrates          c. Harry Potter

    b. Galileo           d. your teacher

**$200 Level**

When you enter class in the morning (or at the beginning of the period), you are to immediately:

    a. Tip the teacher.          c. Face north.

    b. Begin the activity.       d. Finish your homework.

**$500 Level**

Risk-taking in this class is encouraged. *If you never go out on a limb, you'll never get any fruit.* Under each of you is:

    a. the floor          c. a life preserver

    b. a safety net        d. a trap door

**$1,000 Level**

In this classroom:

    a. There are no putdowns.       c. Manners rule.

    b. We care about other people.      d. All of the above

**$8,000 Level**

Inappropriate language in this classroom (and school) will warrant:

    a. an automatic discipline slip      c. a strict warning

    b. a trip to the principal's office      d. a verbal reprimand

**$16,000 Level**

The teacher in this room will be fair and won't always be:

    a. lazy           c. temperamental

    b. unfair          d. equal

## $32,000 Level

For every privilege in this classroom (and in life), there is a:

a. penalty

b. responsibility

c. homework assignment

d. math activity

## $64,000 Level

Substitute teachers in this room are to be treated like:

a. your lost cousin

b. student teachers

c. everyone else

d. special guests

## $125,000 Level

Life skills that we will honor this year in our class include all of the following *except*:

a. respect

b. integrity

c. caring

d. longevity

## $250,000 Level

If I hear your voice over other voices in your group, your voice is considered:

a. rude behavior

b. unacceptable

c. bad noise

d. all of the above

## $500,000 Level

When you "fess up," you:

a. Admit that you're wrong and accept the consequence.

b. Defend yourself, even when you're wrong, by debating the evidence.

c. Find a flaw in the other person's argument.

d. Confess even though you didn't do it.

## $1,000,000 Level

This year will be your greatest school year:

a. since kindergarten

b. because it will be easy

c. of your life

d. because there are only two big exams

# TOPIC 18

# Standards and Expectations

## Examples of School Rules

1. Students will show respect for the rights and property of others.
2. Students will not hurt themselves or others.
3. We will use appropriate language at all times.
4. Students are not permitted in the hallways before or after school without teacher supervision.
5. Chewing gum is not allowed in school.
6. Toys and electronic equipment should not be brought to school.
7. No illegal substances or dangerous weapons may be brought to school.
8. No "sagging" clothing is allowed. Hats are permitted on the playground only.
9. Students should practice "life skills" at all times.

## Example of School Creed

Our school is a caring community.
I am responsible for my actions!
I can learn and support others as they learn.
I will respect the feelings, rights, and property of others!
I must help everyone be safe!

## Examples of Classroom Rules

1. No fighting. Talk it out. Walk away. Give the other person time.
2. Treat others the way you want to be treated.
3. Don't talk when someone else is talking.
4. Talk in a low voice.
5. Show respect for others.
6. Walk in the building.
7. No bad language.

## Secondary School Policies

1. Conduct
2. Participation
3. Materials
4. Cheating
5. Absences
6. Make-up work
7. Late work
8. Tardies
9. Passes

**What?** Standards are rules, policies, and governing laws that are established the first day/week of school or *before* every *new* activity.

**Why?** Without standards (clear expectations), students are free to set their own, often unacceptable, limits of behavior.

**How?** Establish a concerted teacher effort to "train the students" during the first critical days of school or before a *new* activity. This will pay huge dividends throughout the year. Be sure all rules, policies, and expectations are prominently displayed in classrooms and hallways.

# Classroom Welcome Sign

This is a great classroom sign to enlarge, laminate, and place near the classroom door.

**W**hen you

**E**nter this classroom of

**L**imitless opportunities

**C**onsider yourself

**O**ne of the very special

**M**embers of our community and

**E**njoy learning and working together

# Teacher Oath

This is another great classroom sign to enlarge, laminate, and place on the wall of your room. The first week of school establishes the philosophy of the statement. The explanation will prevent disagreements when students complain they are being treated "unfairly."

"I will be fair, AND I won't always be equal."

**TEACHER OATH**

*I will always listen to your explanation or your side of the story.*

*Because life can be unpredictable and unfair, consequences or penalties will depend on ALL information and circumstances.*

*You will not always be treated equally.*

*Some decisions are private and will not be shared with the class.*

*I will attempt to be as fair as humanly possible.*

# Procedure + Practice = Routine*

1. entering        7. end of period
2. responding      8. groups
3. papers          9. papers
4. visitors       10. discussions
5. firedrills     11. attention
6. working        12. announce

practice —
    practice —
        practice!

ROUTINE

| **What?** | Procedures are for training students to accomplish routine tasks in the classroom. |
|---|---|
| **Why?** | Without procedures and routines, a great deal of time is lost through inefficient activity and movement. |

**How?**

1. Tell students exactly what to do, and then model an example (dry run). These training sessions include:

   - entering the classroom
   - responding to questions
   - passing in papers
   - having visitors in the classroom
   - responding to fire drills
   - getting to work immediately

   - end of the period
   - changing groups
   - heading on papers
   - participating in class discussions
   - coming to attention
   - P.A. announcements

2. Practice immediately with the students. The procedure then becomes an automatic routine.

3. If students backslide, practice again with the students.

*Terms by Harry Wong, author of *The First Days of School*

# Rules of Never and Always

NEVER          ALWAYS

| | |
|---|---|
| **What?** | Rules of Never and Always are established the first day/week of school. They are absolutes that are strictly required of every student. |
| **Why?** | Rules of Never and Always set student boundaries and habits that ensure safety and attention to classroom rules and requirements. |
| **How?** | Explain and post the Rules of Never and Always the first day/week of school, and review the rules as needed. |

Examples of Rules of Never and Always might include:

## Never

- Hurt anyone.
- Cheat: Don't do it!
- Bring food or gum to class without permission.
- Put down another student's contributions.

## Always

- Come prepared to school.
- Participate fully and be an active listener.
- Be punctual.
- Use common courtesy in class.
- Complete the board work upon entering the room.
- Use appropriate language.
- Show respect and tolerance to fellow classmates.
- Follow directions.

*Note:* The items listed are samples. They would, of course, vary with each teacher and his/her unique setting and school.

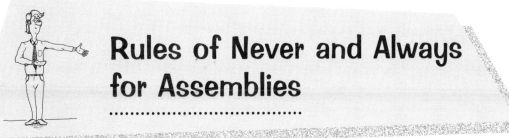

# Rules of Never and Always for Assemblies

## For Teachers:

### Never

1. Seat "Billy the Kid" next to "Attila the Hun."
2. Leave another teacher to "watch" your class.
3. Leave for the assembly without reviewing standards of behavior.

### Always

1. Prep students for the program.
2. Establish behavior expectations. (See rules below.)
3. Have an assembly on assemblies (a dry run) to establish a routine that students will follow on the day of the real thing.
4. Praise, reinforce, and celebrate good behavior.
5. Review the reason and benefits of assembly programs.
6. Model appropriate applause.

## For Students:

### Never

1. Make a choice to sit next to a friend who may be a "problem."
2. Bring ANYTHING to the assembly unless directed by the teacher. No food, gum, drinks, pencils, etc., are permitted.

### Always

1. Pay strict attention to the speaker.
2. Respect the guest speaker(s).
3. Listen and learn.
4. Promptly respond to directions from teachers or the principal.

# Danger Rule

| | |
|---|---|
| **What?** | This is a rule that is established for clearly defining when a student can physically defend him- or herself from a bully. |
| **Why?** | Many kids do not have a clear understanding of when to defend themselves. Very often home and school guidelines in this area are lacking ("Just hit him a good one if he bothers you."). Therefore, a specific rule/procedure is required. |
| **How?** | Say and post: "The biggest rule in this classroom/school is that no one can hurt you, and you cannot hurt anyone else. The only time you can physically defend yourself is when you are in DANGER." |

Use class discussion time to clearly delineate the "danger" situations. Here is a sample class discussion:

| Teacher | Student response | Teacher response |
|---|---|---|
| 1. "Are you in danger if a person calls you a bad name?" | "No." | "Then you are not in danger." |
| 2. "Are you in danger if a student bumps you at the water fountain?" | "No." | "Then you are not in danger." |
| 3. "Are you in danger if two kids hit you and jump on you on the playing field?" | "Yes." | "Then you may defend yourself **ONLY UNTIL THE DANGER IS OVER.**" |

# "Fess Up" Rule

**What?** The "fess up" rule is explained to students the first day of school. It invites students to "confess" to an infraction of rules or standards of acceptable behavior.

**Why?** The "fess up" rule promotes and encourages student responsibility for their actions.

**How?** Tell students that a rule violation or misbehavior followed by a lie or an attempted coverup only magnifies the dilemma and the consequence will then become more severe. But, if the students "fess up" and admit the transgression, then the consequence is usually less severe.

Lead a classroom discussion of how "fessing up" occurs in real life and in our legal system.

# Classroom Rules Checklist

| | |
|---|---|
| **What?** | The *classroom rules checklist* guides you in establishing a system that helps to control classroom behavior. |
| **Why?** | This checklist enables you to establish order early in the year and eliminates many problem situations before they start. |
| **How?** | Check all items that apply on the checklist. (See the sample checklist below.) |

In my classroom, I:

☐ Limit classroom rules to about four or five.

☐ Post rules and refer to them by number as needed or in group discussions.

☐ Involve students in making rules (no involvement, no commitment).

☐ Reinforce students for following rules (catch them being good).

☐ Communicate consequences of not following the rules.

☐ Stop inappropriate behavior, language, or movement immediately.

☐ Am consistent as humanly possible.

☐ Clearly tell students what is inappropriate and how to correct it.

☐ Am conscious that the majority of interactions throughout the day/year should be positive in nature and are tantamount to a successful year.

☐ Establish a culture of trust and appreciation.

☐ Am aware of different options or choices connected with students' behavior.

☐ Strive to make learning a genuinely pleasurable activity.

# Safety Net

| | |
|---|---|
| **What?** | The *safety net* concept promotes risk-taking and self-reliance in the classroom. |
| **Why?** | Risk-taking student behavior is valued by most classroom teachers. The "safety net" philosophy encourages and rewards risk-taking. |
| **How?** | Establish the "safety net" class policy the first week of school. |

TEACHER: How many of you have seen a person on a trapeze? Good. Most of these performers have a net under them in case they fall. It's called a *safety net* and it's used to make sure that no one is injured. This year I want to encourage you to be free-thinkers and risk-takers. I want you to exercise your wonderful brains in creative ways. Therefore, I will be rewarding you for creative thinking. And just as important, no one is permitted to put you down for your statements and opinions. They will not mock you for exercising your brain. That is your safety net. It's okay to jump, be a risk-taker, because you can't and won't get hurt. I won't put you down and no one else will either.

## Important Points:

1. Assertively reinforce the "safety net" concept the first week of school.
2. Come down hard on violators.
3. Use and review "Higher-Level Thinking Skills" (Topic 68).
4. Reward convergent/divergent thinking throughout the year.
5. Verbally reinforce and highlight "out of the box" thinking.

# Privileges and Responsibilities

| | |
|---|---|
| **What?** | The idea of *privileges and responsibilities* is an excellent reminder to students of an important life skill. |
| **Why?** | You connect privileges in the classroom and in life with accompanying responsibilities. This is a great life skill lesson for all students. |
| **How?** | Take every opportunity to build your students' responsibilities. |

TEACHER: With most privileges in life, there are connected responsibilities. I have the privilege of being able to drive my car anywhere in the country, but I must be a responsible driver by following the rules and laws.

TEACHER: You have the privilege to sit next to your friend. What is the responsibility?
STUDENT: To not disturb the class.
TEACHER: Excellent! However, if you do, I will have to separate you."

TEACHER: Today, we have the privilege of attending a special assembly. Who can tell me what our responsibility is?
STUDENT: To behave as a responsible citizen.
TEACHER: Right!

TEACHER: It's field trip day! (Cheers!) We are going to spend the whole day at the science museum with our favorite docents. This is a special privilege, so before we leave, let's review our responsibilities. (See Topic 18 on standards and clear expectations.)

# Briefing

**What?**    A *briefing* is a short meeting at the beginning and/or the end of the school day or period.

**Why?**    The briefing allows for a short class meeting to concisely review the plans and challenges for the day/period. This meeting sets the stage for upcoming lessons and activities, and ultimately saves valuable time throughout the day.

**How?**    Walk the class through the day's plans. Directions and pertinent information are shared with the group. "Monitor" the class to assure that all students understand the challenges of the day. Monitoring includes having several students explain each task before releasing the group to begin. (See Topic 75 on paraphrasing for more help in this area.) The end-of-the-period/-day briefing allows for the group to: review the day's progress, make suggestions for improvement, and preview upcoming challenges and learning activities.

# The Business Face

From the first minute of school, the successful classroom teacher sends a clear message to the total class that: "When you see *this* face, I MEAN BUSINESS!" Examples of class business include such things as the beginning of a lesson or important announcements and directions. TOTAL compliance is the order of the day.

Procedure:

1. Stand in the same area of the room each time.
2. Put on your business face.
3. Use a "laser" stare to command attention from all students.
4. Clear throat if needed.
5. Say "Excuse me" (very indignantly) if needed.
6. Need more power? "I beg your pardon!"
7. Congratulate/thank students for their cooperation.

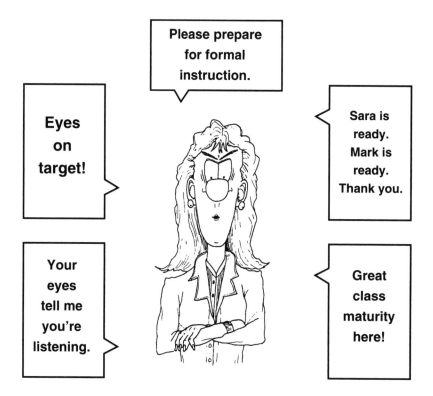

# SECTION 5

# Vocabulary

This section focuses on technical words, quotations, sayings, and expressions that will increase your skills when implementing the techniques and strategies covered in Section 6. Some of the quotations and terms are philosophical in nature, while others can be used directly with students and placed on a classroom wall.

# Great Quotations for Your Classroom

*Read this once and remember it always!*

| Quotation | Application |
|---|---|
| *If the only tool you have is a hammer, you treat everything like a nail.* | The "hammer" is your heavy weapon that is used to demonstrate power and authority. It is a useful tool but should be used sparingly along with many other tools in your toolbox. Adopt many of the new ideas you discover in this book and use a *variety* of tools. |
| *The same boiling water that hardens eggs softens the carrots.* | Techniques that work with some kids don't with others. All the more reason you need many tools in your toolbox. One of the secrets to good classroom control is knowing which approach to use in which situation. |
| *We all guard the gate of change, it is tender holy ground.* | It's difficult to change old habits, but if you gradually incorporate new ideas and techniques into your teaching, you *can* make progress. |
| *If you want different, you have to do different.* | Stop complaining. If you're so miserable, then you have to change your ways. |
| *Episodic knowledge—don't leave home without it.* | Each time there is an exchange or situation with a student, it is registered as an episode. After continued episodes, you become more comfortable, confident, and competent in your decisions. You often click into automatic mode with a response or solution. This occurs because your episodic knowledge allows you to make quick, accurate decisions based on your many and continued experiences. |

*This is great stuff!*

| Quotation | Application |
|---|---|
| "No wonder I'm tired." | Five hundred management decisions a day add up to about a half million a year! This can have an erosive effect on even the best teacher and slowly drain you of valuable energy. The goal is to increase your skills, decrease your management decisions, and sustain your energy over the year AND your career. |
| *If you want power, you have to give it away.* | Establish rules and standards the first week of the year WITH your students. Use the democratic choice technique to empower your students. "You have a choice. You may sit and work quietly with your friends OR you'll have to split up. What would you like to do?" |
| *Give them a soft place to fall.* | Encourage and reward risk-taking. Celebrate "out of the box" thinkers. Never let anyone be put down in the classroom. Reinforce synergistic activity and thinking. See Topic 24, Safety Net, for more information. |
| *Calm is control.* | Realize that your life is in the hands of any fool who makes you lose your temper. |
| *Aggressive consequences are viewed as punishments.* | Consequences condemn the act, not the actor. You must remain calm and "matter of fact." See Topic 31, Kiss of Kisses, for more information. |
| *Do not make a demand that you are not prepared to follow through on.* | This is a common mistake of beginning teachers. If you find you're in a real dilemma and are frustrated, the best thing to do is to evoke the 24-hour rule (see Topic 96) and sleep on it. This gives you an opportunity to regain composure, collect information, talk to your mentor teacher or principal, and make a better decision. Beware of group punishments! |
| *Education is the ability to listen to almost anything without losing your temper.* —Robert Frost | Calm is control. It's not the snake bite that kills you; it's running like a madman that drives the poison to your heart. Calm is control. |
| *When a teacher calls a boy by his entire name, it means trouble.* —Mark Twain | TEACHER: (referring to a boy who is in trouble) Quincy Adams!!! |

In later life,

as in earlier,

only a few persons influence the formation of our

character;

the multitude pass us by like a distant army.

One friend,

one teacher,

one beloved,

one club,

one dining table are the means by which one's nation

and the spirit of one's nation

affect the individual.

JEAN PAUL RICHTER

# Interventions

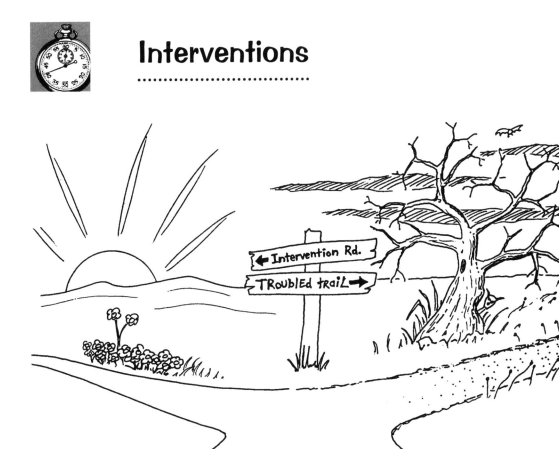

| What? | Interventions are positive approaches used to change a behavior. Examples of interventions are a behavior plan, a contract, and a behavior-modification technique. |
|---|---|
| Why? | If you don't intervene, the student's behavior does not improve. |
| How? | Use any of the following interventions or those of your own: |

- Parent conference
- Referral to child study team
- Review of child's office folder
- Information from previous teacher(s)
- Behavior contracts (See Topic 107.)
- Advice from specialists (psychologist, speech therapist, etc.)
- Referral for testing
- Assistance from an outside agency
- Advice from mentor/master teacher

# Sins of Omission

Anytime you think the problem is "out there," *that* is the problem.

**What?** At times, teachers feel overwhelmed by the problem(s) that students bring to school. Teachers rationalize the situation and place blame on lack of parenting skills, single-parent families, society, TV, and so on. These are sins of omission.

**Why?** Teachers must constantly search for answers to the challenges presented by their students. Anything less is unacceptable. This is a profession that lights candles to dispel the darkness.

**How?** Avoid sins of omission by doing the following:

1. Read the cumulative folder and check with past teachers.
2. Meet with parent(s) and inside professionals.
3. Meet with parent(s) and outside professionals.
4. Create an action contract. (See Topic 107 for several samples.)
5. Trade the challenging student for another student from another teacher. This gives each teacher and student a new start and hopefully an improved situation for all.
6. Refer to the school's child study team for assistance and/or testing.

# In-School Suspensions

**What?** In-school suspension is a form of isolation that removes the offending student (serious violations) from the classroom.

**Why?** In-school suspension exiles the student from the class. This last-resort strategy sends a clear message to the perpetrator and other students that misbehavior will not be tolerated. It restores order and clears the way for relatively uninterrupted instruction.

**How?** Many schools (especially secondary) have detention rooms for suspended students. Successful schools have procedures for excluding students that teachers and administrators have set up. Successful suspension rooms must have established procedures and standards for student conduct. Teachers and administrators also need to set guidelines as to when to exclude a student from class. This technique is generally most effective as a LAST resort.

Some elementary teachers could use the lunch-hour recess time as an in-house suspension time, where teachers take turns throughout the week being on "guard duty." This minimizes the time an individual teacher has to be on duty. Once more, standards and procedures are tantamount to success.

# Mistaken Goals of Misbehavior*

| | |
|---|---|
| **What?** | The *mistaken goals of misbehavior* identify some reasons or motivations for discipline problems. |
| **Why?** | If you understand the reason for misbehavior, you can attempt strategies to manage that behavior. |
| **How?** | Read the four goals listed below with possible strategies for alleviating the problem(s). |

## Getting Attention

- Focus on catching kids being good.
- Ignore!
- Do not nag, coax, or scold. (That's what they want!)
- Give attention to "good" kids.

## Looking for Power

- "I can't continue without your cooperation."
- Use the pregnant pause. (See Topic 46.)
- "Do you think you could help by setting an example?"
- Don't get into power struggles or win–lose situations. (You must withdraw and thwart the purpose of power-seeking behavior.)

## Seeking Revenge

- Get another student to assist you with the perpetrator.
- Use class pressure on the perpetrator.

## Displaying Inadequacy

- Encourage and support the student.
- Don't indicate defeat or frustration to the student.
- Provide success at the student's level and react positively.

*Term by Rudolf Dreikurs, co-author of *Maintaining Sanity in the Classroom*

# Baci di Tutti Bocci
## ("kiss of all kisses")

REMAIN IN CONTROL...

**What?** The *kiss of all kisses* is your unemotional response to a student who has broken an important rule. (Remember the movie *Godfather, Part II* when Michael Corleone unemotionally kisses his brother "goodbye" because he betrayed the family?)

**Why?** Your unemotional response to a broken rule or inappropriate behavior condemns the sin, not the sinner. It also demonstrates that you are in control. *Calm equals control!* If you are in control, it minimizes the chance of your saying or doing something you will later regret. "My life is in the hands of any fool who makes me lose my temper."

**How?** Clearly articulate the infraction and give the student ample opportunity to tell his or her side of the story (due process). If the student is found guilty, the mutual consequence plan (see Topic 32) is then initiated.

# The Mutual Consequence Plan

**What?** The *mutual consequence plan* enables the offender to take ownership in the transgression.

**Why?** The consequence is then mutually agreed upon by both parties and is not the sole burden of the teacher. Generally, students are very realistic in suggesting fair and appropriate consequences.

**How?** Say: "You did the crime and now you have to pay the time. Tell you what I'm going to do. I want you to go home and return tomorrow with three possible *written* consequences. I will pick one of yours, or help you fine-tune one of yours with you, or give you one of my own."

The student now has to go home and sweat out the situation alone or with his or her parents. The burden is now on the perpetrator. This "let 'em sweat" technique goes a long way in assuring that the infraction will not be repeated.

# Good and Bad Noise or Movement

**What?**   You use this technique to moderate/control the noise/movement level in the classroom.

**Why?**   The noise level or movement in a classroom during an activity can often get out of control and become detrimental to instruction.

**How?**   Explain to the class that bad noise/movement infringes on the rights of others. Then say, "If I can hear YOUR voice OVER the other voices in your group, then it is BAD noise. If I can't hear any ONE voice, it is good noise." Likewise, "If your movement infringes on the rights of others, it is BAD movement. If not, it is GOOD movement." This technique helps students moderate their voices and movements.

# Grandma's Law

| | |
|---|---|
| **What?** | *Grandma's law* is "You must eat your meal before you get your dessert." |
| **Why?** | Students are motivated to complete a task if they know there is a "payoff." |
| **How?** | Grandma's law is especially useful when the group's morale is slipping. Your reminder of the "dessert" keeps the group motivated and on task. Smart teachers save "dessert"—such as field trips, guest speakers, and special activities—for the last weeks of the school year or semester. |

# Techniques, Strategies, and Good Ideas

This section offers 15 easy-to-use support ideas, which can be quickly added to your "bag of tricks." Reviewing this section on a regular basis will gradually become a natural part of your day and increase your skill in handling behavior problems.

*A teacher*
*affects eternity;*
*he can never tell*
*where*
*his influence*
*stops.*

HENRY BROOK ADAMS

# "Pick a Card, Any Card"

**What?**    This activity offers two decks of cards: one for consequences and one for rewards. The cards provide a way to intervene with minor behavior problems (consequences) or positively reward student behavior (reward).

**Why?**    Because this idea relates to all students, they view the cards as fair. The students also understand that:

- If you do the crime, you pay the time.
- Good behavior and good deeds are accepted here.

**How?**    Have the students participate in selecting the consequences and the rewards that go on the cards. Also add your own items to the cards. The offending/rewarded student then picks a card from the appropriate deck and serves the consequence or accepts the reward.

# Reward Cards

Use a regular deck of cards (or index cards) and paste (or print) reward ideas on the cards. The following card samples are a start . . . use your imagination for more ideas. When a student qualifies (this is also up to you), he or she draws a card and receives his or her "payoff."

| | | |
|---|---|---|
| 1 point toward Friday class party (5 points required) | First out to lunch or dismissal for one week | One-day homework excuse pass |
| Free paperback book | Choice of seat on bus for next field trip | Super seat (seat of honor) for one week |
| **5** bonus homework points | Video-party video picker | 1 point toward class pizza party (5 points required) |
| Lunch with the teacher and a friend | **5** bonus test points | **Free lunch** |
| 15-minute game period for the entire class | **10** minutes of background music of your choice. G-rated! | Free snack from snack jar |

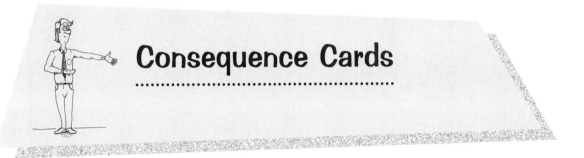

# Consequence Cards

Use a regular deck of cards (or index cards) and paste (or print) consequence ideas on the cards. The following card samples are a start . . . use your imagination for more ideas. When a student qualifies (this is also up to you), he or she draws a card and receives his or her "duty" assignment.

| | | |
|---|---|---|
| **1** point off class 15-minute chitchat time | Write a one-page paper concerning your rule violation. How are you going to remedy the situation so it doesn't happen again? | **Stop!** Time out for one hour. |
| **1** hour in buddy teacher's timeout room | Last out to lunch for one week | Phone call to parent(s). Teacher reports "situation" and student reports commitment to change. |
| Clean/polish super seat and area for one week | Litter police. Get basket and clean up floor. | No bonus homework points this week |
| **Dust the room!** | Spend the next movie in buddy teacher's timeout room. | Last out for dismissal for one week |
| **1** point off class party | Spend the next party in buddy teacher's timeout room. | Spend next recess next to teacher. |
| Spend next recess in buddy teacher's room. | Free autographed picture of your teacher. | **5** laps around school field at recess |

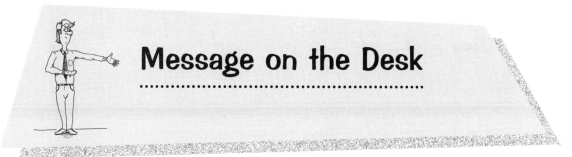

# Message on the Desk

1. Keep a supply of silent messages (below) available.

2. Without interrupting instruction, move to the offender or praisee and place the message on the desk.

3. The frowning face and smiling face mean that there will be a one-on-one student–teacher "meeting" after the lesson.

4. The frowning telephone message is more serious and may result in a call home. The smiling telephone message means you want to share the good news with parents.

5. You may want to use the first frowning face as a warning and allow the student to tear it up if there are no repeat violations.

This is an excellent idea for reinforcing positive effort and attitude. Use sincere, legitimate praise:

TEACHER: Why do you think I gave you that smiling face?
STUDENT: Because I made an excellent effort in completing the paper?
TEACHER: Bingo!

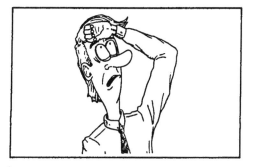

# Visual Cues

| | |
|---|---|
| **What?** | *Visual cues* are nonverbal messages sent from you to the students. |
| **Why?** | During the course of the school day, kids are often overwhelmed with verbal commands and cues. Visual cues are a refreshing way of telling students what you want them to do. Generally, they also do not solicit a response. This avoids the typical verbal combat that can often occur when you direct the pupil. Visual cues are also easier on you, by saving energy. |
| **How?** | Use hand signals, such as those described below. |

**Important note:** Do not speak when using visual cues!

| Signal | What it conveys to students |
|---|---|
| Index finger pointed | "Not now" or "Wait a minute." |
| Hand palm raised | "Stop!" |
| Index finger to lips | "Be quiet!" |
| Thumb up | "You're doing great!" |
| Head shake | "No, don't do that!" |
| Zip lips | "Be quiet!" |
| Finger-snapping | "Attention!" |
| Finger on nose | "Correct answer (right on the nose)" |
| Index finger curling | "Come here, we need to talk." |
| Index finger waving | "No, no, no!" |
| Nod, smile, pat on the back | "Keep up the great work!" |

SUPPORT IDEA

## "Your Eyes Tell Me You Are Listening"

The following procedure will bring your class to attention and have all students focus on you.

1. Show the "Your eyes tell me you are listening" look.
2. *Wait* for total compliance.
3. Do *not* begin speaking until *all eyes are on you*.

# Proximity Control

| **What?** | *Proximity control* finds you moving near or next to the student(s) who is misbehaving or disrupting instruction. |
|---|---|
| **Why?** | Your presence near the misbehaving student has a "chilling effect" on that student. Research indicates that the closer you are to student(s), the fewer the discipline problems. |
| **How?** | Continue instruction and *without speaking* move next to (near) the offending student or group of students. |

**Note:** Low-level intervention to higher-level interventions may be needed. Once compliance (students are doing what you want them to do) is achieved, you can move out. In some cases, you should "hang around" to ensure compliance. Most interventions work at the very low levels (1, 2, or 3).

Level 1.   Move to student.
Level 2.   Take two relaxed breaths (no teacher words).
Level 3.   Use visual signals (Topic 36) to direct student.
Level 4.   Say (quietly and indignantly) "Excuse me."
Level 5.   Lean one palm on student's desk and tell exactly what to do.
Level 6.   Lean two palms on student's desk and tell exactly what to do.
Level 7.   Use private appeal (Topic 38).
Level 8.   Say "See me after class."
Level 9.   Exclude from group (*last resort*) as per class or school policy.

# Private (Direct) Appeal

**What?** The *direct appeal* has you asking the student to step into the hall (you can still see the class) where a one-on-one private discussion can take place.

**Why?** The private (direct) appeal removes the culprit from his or her audience. It also has a chilling effect (ripple effect) on the rest of the class.

**How?** Calmly ask the student to explain the situation. After you hear the story, you have the option to: empathize, condemn the behavior, invite cooperation, outline the consequences of future misbehavior, arrange for a future meeting, reprimand, etc. Generally, the technique is enhanced if you whisper. (Calm is control.)

# One-Minute Correction

**What?**   The *one-minute correction* is a procedure for reprimanding a student for unacceptable behavior.

**Why?**   When necessary, students need to be aware that there are consequences of their misbehavior. They also must understand that you are a positive, support person who is there to assist them in improving future behavior.

**How?**
1. During the first week of school, explain to students that if they break the rules, they will be held accountable.

2. Reprimand immediately if a rule is broken!

3. Immediately tell what the student had done wrong.

4. Tell the student how you feel.

5. Pause . . . and let it sink in.

6. Remind the student that you value him or her and that you are on his or her side. Condemn the sin, *not* the sinner.

7. Upon leaving the meeting with the student, let the reprimand stand without a "softening" gesture. The goal here is to send a clear message to the offender and strengthen the impact of the reprimand.

# Encouraging Effort

- Reinforce correct answers.
- Verbally reward first efforts.
- Help students learn from mistakes and get better.

TEACHER:  Class, is it all right to make mistakes?
STUDENTS: Yes.
TEACHER:  Why?
STUDENTS: Because we're learning!

- Lead students to the next goal or challenge.
- Reinforce correct areas of work.
- Explore other ways or possibilities to accomplish the task.
- Celebrate (individual and group) progress and task completion.

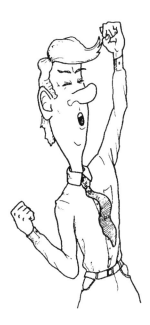

# TWWA

| | |
|---|---|
| **What?** | Teaching while walking around, or TWWA. |
| **Why?** | Your proximity improves academic growth and enhances management skills. |
| **How?** | Move from student to student or desk to desk. You are then able to: encourage, reteach, let your presence be felt, manipulate group dynamics, monitor and adjust instruction, act as a cheerleader (ripple effect), pressure, meet privately with individual students, and more. |

# Seating Arrangements

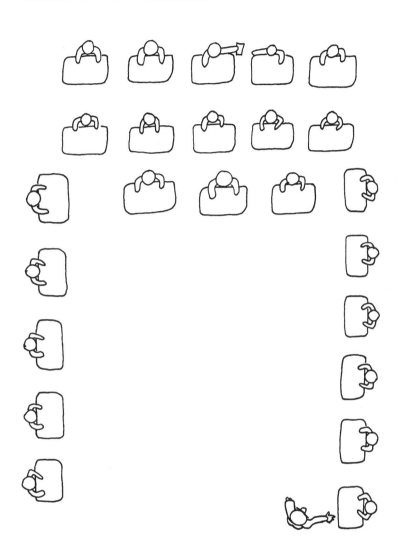

| | |
|---|---|
| **What?** | The seating arrangement is the placement of seats, chairs, or tables in a classroom. |
| **Why?** | The placement of students' seats is used as a positive asset in controlling student behavior. |
| **How?** | There are as many seating arrangements as there are teachers. However, you should strive for a setup that allows you to get *to* students (see Topic 37, Proximity Control) as easily as possible. The closer you are to the students, the fewer the problems. When possible, a U-shaped arrangement lends itself to easy access to students. |

# Separate "Problem" Kids

We learn from group dynamics that kids act and react differently when alone, with a friend, or in a group. Behavior "problems" seem amazingly adept at finding each other. They find each other in class, on the playground, and at assemblies.

Use your teacher wisdom to see which of the following suggested strategies work in your unique situation:

1. Share the power. Tell the "high risk" pair that they may sit together provided they do not disturb the lesson or their neighbors.

   TEACHER:   The choice you have is to sit together and behave or you will not be permitted to sit next to each other. What would you like to do?

2. Tell the "problem" kids they are NEVER to sit together.

3. Assign seats next to you at an assembly or when a guest speaker is in your classroom.

4. Assign bus and destination seats on a field trip.

Timeout With
a Buddy Teacher

1. Give the student the choice of exhibiting acceptable behavior *or* moving to a specified timeout seat/area. Give a warning that a repeat of the poor behavior will warrant a trip to the classroom of your buddy teacher. If all goes well, the student returns to the classroom after a short period.

2. If the unacceptable behavior continues, have the student escorted to the timeout classroom by a dependable student(s).

3. The receiving teacher should coolly direct (with few words) the student to the private, designated timeout area of the classroom. The student is persona non grata and should not be recognized or noticed by the other kids. These brief sessions away from the home classroom are most effective.

4. Try to use a buddy teacher at a two- or three-grade (spread) distance. For example, a second-grade teacher sends to a fifth-grade teacher and vice versa.

# Trading Places

As the year progresses, it becomes evident that, as hard as many teachers try, the student–teacher relationship isn't working. Trading places is an exchange of "problem" kids. Teachers mutually agree, *with principal and parent approval*, to switch students. Many times this gives all parties a fresh start, and hopefully an improved situation for all.

Lots of good communication among all participants should be the order of the day.

# The Consequence Fits the Crime

| | |
|---|---|
| **What?** | Consequences must fit the crime. You (and parents) must see that consequences are reasonable, age appropriate, and in the best interest of the student. |
| **Why?** | Unrealistic punishments or threats serve little purpose. You should not make a demand that you are not prepared to follow through on. |
| **How?** | Use Topic 32, the Mutual Consequence Plan. |

# 90/10 Rule

| **What?** | Interactions (verbal exchanges between you and students) should be positive in nature. If one were to measure those interactions, they should be approximately 90% positive and 10% negative. |
| --- | --- |
| **Why?** | Building rapport and positive relationships is tantamount to success in teaching. Teachers who establish this positive classroom atmosphere promote learning and a positive learning environment. |
| **How?** | Focus your attention on reinforcing behavior and standards. This reminds students of classroom principles, listed below. |

"I can always count on you to be responsible."
"I appreciate the way you helped your classmate."
"It was great the way you returned to work after we had that good laugh.
   Your maturity is showing."
"What a terrific thinker!"
"Great teamwork! Much appreciation."
"I think you guys are ready for next year."
"The room looks just great. Thanks for your cooperation."
"You demonstrated excellent maturity at the assembly."
"I appreciate your leadership and teamwork."

# Voice Control

**What?**   Voice control enables you to use your voice as a teaching tool.

**Why?**   Use your voice:

- for dramatic effect
- to command attention
- to save energy throughout the day/year
- to model and establish a climate that is conducive to good mental health

**How?**
1. Lower (whisper level) your voice to emphasize a point.

2. Raise (above direct instruction) your voice to emphasize a point.

3. Your volume level should be appropriate to the situation. A level slightly above your speaking voice should be used for direct instruction. A voice that is too loud for the situation wastes valuable teacher energy over the course of a day and year.

4. One-to-one assistance should be done in a whisper-level voice. This assists you for when you need to command attention; you need only to increase your volume. It also saves valuable energy.

# Questions and Requests

Make requests close (3 feet) to students.

Use a low voice and give them the laser look.

Do not ask kids to start work . . . TELL them.

Make a request and give them 4 or 5 seconds to respond.

Give one request at a time and then wait for compliance.

# The Laser Stare
# (or "The Look")

**What?** The laser stare or "the look" is a disapproving look from you to the student.

**Why?** The laser stare enables you to control behavior by simply looking (no words) at an offending student. The stare saves energy and usually does not require a response from the student. Student responses often lead to unnecessary, and time-wasting, back-and-forth exchanges between you and the student.

**How?** Boldly give your most authoritative look (stance and body language) directly at the offending student. If required, a visual cue (see Topic 36) can be added. Use no words and demand compliance before "releasing" the stare (once the student complies). An optional compliment can also be made, such as "Thanks for your cooperation."

# Interruptions

On any given day, you are confronted with all kinds of interruptions. P.A. announcements and kids leaving for special classes, lessons, the nurse, and doctors' appointments are all among the potential distractions throughout the school day.

Because interruptions are a fact of classroom life, a proactive approach to the problem is as follows:

1. NEVER allow kids to talk over P.A. announcements. Sure, some of the announcements may be annoying and irrelevant, but to allow the students to talk over them is disrespectful and poor modeling.

2. Practice the listening procedure the first day of school.

3. Review and practice a dry run on how to quietly leave and enter the classroom.

4. Verbally praise good listeners.

5. Reward good listeners.

6. Use the echo technique to have selected students repeat important announcements for the class (reward as needed).

7. Practice and use the following procedure to refocus your class after an interruption.

TEACHER: We will be visiting the museum on Friday. The docent will meet us at the entrance and we will proceed to the indoor theater for a review of the day's activities. Please remember to bring your journals and the questions for the . . .

P.A. ANNOUNCEMENT: Please excuse the interruption. Band practice is canceled today and the Girl Scouts will meet in the cafeteria at 3:00. Thank you.

TEACHER: Very good. Who is brave enough to summarize what I was saying about the field trip before the office announcement?

STUDENT: (Debbie summarizes the field trip information.)

TEACHER: Very good, Debbie. You get a 5-point test bonus coupon.

**Note:** If you establish this procedure after each interruption, the routine will result in a minimum of lost time.

# The Pregnant Pause

**What?**   The *pregnant pause* finds you standing silently at the front of the class with a very concerned expression on your face.

**Why?**   The pregnant pause sends a visual message (no words) to the class that complete silence is now required.

**How?**   Stand silently at the front of the class with an indignant look on your face. You may want to use the laser stare or "the look" (see Topic 45). Send a visual message to the class that you *mean business*. Wait for *total* group compliance before speaking. Once compliance is achieved, compliment the class for its cooperation. The pregnant pause will quickly become an established routine (see Topic 19).

You can use escalations ("up the stakes") for noncompliance situations:

Level 1.   Clear your throat (but still no talking) and use a face that tells the class "I mean business!"

Level 2.   After several seconds, say (indignantly) "Excuse me!" This usually does it.

Level 3.   Review procedure for the pregnant pause or reestablish routine.

# "See Me After Class"

| | |
|---|---|
| **What?** | "See me after class" is a technique for dealing with disruptive students who don't respond to earlier teacher attempts at eliminating the disruption. |
| **Why?** | "See me after class" has a chilling effect on students. One consequence to the student is the reduction of socialization time between classes or after school. |
| **How?** | Tell the student (whisper level) "See me after class." Then when the student meets with you, stall (using the student's social time) by doing paperwork. Then finally discuss the situation with the offending student. This strong negative consequence has a future ripple effect. Whisper level is important because it generally does not solicit a student response. |

# Broken Record

No, not ever.

Absolutely not.

No, you may not.

You may not do that.

That is not allowed.

No.... NO.

| | |
|---|---|
| **What?** | The *broken-record* technique stipulates that you assertively repeat the message or command that must be obeyed by the student. |
| **Why?** | The broken-record technique can most often be used when a student is on the verge of "losing it." Remain calm in an attempt to discourage or sidetrack the oncoming storm. |
| **How?** | Calmly repeat a request, with empathy, to cease and desist:<br>"You may not fight in class."<br>"I know you're upset, but you cannot fight here."<br>"I understand, but fighting is out of the question."<br>"Absolutely no fighting. Let's have a seat so we can talk." |

# Study Buddies

**What?**  This is a system whereby each student is assigned a classmate buddy.

**Why?**  You gain tremendous leverage by delegating many tasks and responsibilities to students. Delegate! Delegate! Delegate! This enables you to concentrate on more important tasks and saves valuable teacher energy and stamina. Students teaching other students is also an excellent mutual learning experience.

**How?**  Each student is assigned or picks (your option) a study buddy the first week of school. The kids are told that these partnerships are not in concrete and may change during the year at your discretion.

Study buddies can be responsible for such things as:

1. Maintaining the Class Aid Box (see Topic 83).

2. Informing/updating their buddy of assignments if they are out of the room or absent.

3. Tutoring their study buddy.

4. Calling their study buddy with homework questions or for assistance.

5. Supporting their buddy in the event of illness.

# Bonus Coupons

**What?** Bonus coupons are used to reinforce and reward acceptable behavior and academic progress.

**Why?** Bonus coupons are used to catch kids being good. They also reinforce the concept of promoting a positive classroom climate.

**How?** Prepare bonus coupons. Examples are listed below. Use your imagination for more and ask the class for their input. Students may submit coupons or attach to tests.

- 1 Day of Grace (an extension on due date for an assignment)
- 1 Free Answer Pass (remove one test question)
- 5 Points on a Test
- 10 Points on a Test
- "Pick a Card, Any Card" (consequence reduced by one-half)
- 1 Homework Excuse
- Special Movie Admittance

**Suggestion:** Have a larger number of smaller reward coupons, thereby raising the value of the other coupons.

# Rewards

In any given group of teachers, there is always the debate about rewarding students for "every little thing they do." Teachers appear to be better at extrinsic reinforcement than intrinsic rewarding. Some authors believe that token economies are a negative influence on managing classroom behavior.

However, if you visit most schools in this country, you will see teachers rewarding kids for appropriate behavior and for academic achievement. It is not my purpose here to get into a philosophical debate, but to provide support ideas and information for those teachers who are successful and comfortable using a reward system.

The list below was collected from kids when asked how they would like to spend their "dollars." The list is endless . . . use your great teacher imagination to add to or create your own list.

| Reward Ideas (Collected from kids) | Number of "Dollars" (Suggested payoff price; totally your option) |
|---|---|
| Go to the front of the cafeteria line | 3 |
| Tell a joke on the P.A. (screen all jokes) | 2 |
| Lunch with the principal | 5 |
| Front-row seat at an assembly | 3 |
| Homework excuse pass | 6 |
| Personal teacher assistant for a day | 4 |
| Private computer time (30 minutes) | 4 |
| Special movie (library of class) | 6 |
| Free book | 7 |
| Lunch with a friend and the teacher | 6 |
| Library pass (one hour) | 4 |
| Free reading period (30 minutes) | 3 |
| Class cookie/popcorn party | 20 |
| Choice of seat on bus for a week | 5 |

## What Are We Trying to Do Here?

If you refer to the ways that children can be rewarded, you see that the goal is to encourage character development, namely, to promote:

- mutual respect
- the capacity to think, feel, and act with principles
- democratic participation
- proper social behavior and personal achievement
- the development of self-esteem
- concern for others
- kindness, honesty, responsibility, and respect for others

# Class Auction

1. Establish a reward system for such things as:
   - completing work
   - helping others
   - doing routine tasks
   - being a positive role model
   - supporting life-skills program
   - showing positive behavior
   - any other ideas you want to reinforce

2. Reward students based on above system by giving out class "dollars," tokens, chips, stars, etc.

3. Have students bring (from home) their old (discarded) treasures such as trading cards, games, toys, CDs, posters, books, comics, etc. As the items arrive, place them on a table for all to see. "One person's trash is another person's treasure."

4. When you've collected all the items, hold up an object and have the students use their tokens to bid and buy it.

# 3 Before Me

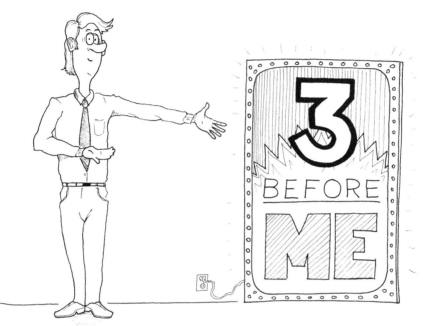

| | |
|---|---|
| **What?** | This activity is a technique used by students to get assistance from classmates. |
| **Why?** | The goals of 3 Before Me are to: |

- Improve listening skills.
- Build self-reliance.
- Promote a spirit of cooperation.
- Assist kids in finding their own answers using visual cues.

| | |
|---|---|
| **How?** | Introduce the students to the system during the first week of school. Encourage the students to "find the answer *without* the teacher" by using the 3 Before Me technique that you have written on a permanent chart. |

---

### 3 Before Me

1. Ask your study buddy.
2. Where can you find the answer in the room (chart, worksheet, bulletin board, etc.)?
3. Ask someone else.

# Noise-Level Control

- SILENCE
- WHISPER LEVEL
- TABLE VOICES

**What?** *Noise-level control* is a visual aid used to establish the acceptable talking level for each activity.

**Why?** Standards are required for all classroom activities. This assists you in establishing a healthy and enjoyable classroom learning climate.

**How?** Make a chart (see below) and, *prior* to beginning the activity or assignment, set the noise-level indicator based on the nature of the activity.

TEACHER: As you can see from our noise-level controller, this is a whisper-level or buddy-voice activity. Please show me what that would sound like. (Kids then demonstrate.) Very good. You may begin.

---

### Noise-Level Indicators

1. Silence (and in seats)
2. Whisper or buddy talking
3. Table voices

# Say the Secret Word/Phrase and All Is Quiet

The secret word/phrase is a fun way of commanding attention in the classroom. Establish the procedure as follows:

1. Each day ask a different student to give the class the secret word or phrase for that day.

2. Put the word or phrase on the board.

3. When you say the secret word/phrase, every student is to FACE YOU AND FREEZE.

4. Use the secret word ONLY when you need students' absolute attention. (**Note:** If the word/phrase is overused, it will lose its effectiveness.)

5. Then share the important information with the students.

6. Repeat the word/phrase to RELEASE the students to return to their work or activity.

# Sandwich Technique

| | |
|---|---|
| **What?** | The *sandwich technique* is a three-step feedback response given to a student. |
| **Why?** | This is another positive reinforcement technique that rewards students and—at the same time—gently invites them to grow. |
| **How?** | Use two positive reinforcement statements with a suggestion placed in the middle. |

"That is exactly right."
"You may want to rethink that statement."
"I think that section is terrific."

"The first row is correct."
"Number 12 needs work."
"The rest looks great."

"I can rely on you to always be helpful."
"I'd appreciate more help in this area."
"I'm very proud of your effort."

# Personal "Gofer"

**What?** Your personal assistant or "gofer" (go for this, go get me that) is a designated student who personally assists you each day.

**Why?** There is always a student in the class with an abundance of energy. The personal assistant idea is a proactive approach to helping this student positively release some of that pent-up energy.

**How?** The "gofer" is delegated a number of classroom jobs/tasks (use your imagination) and is kept busy and occupied throughout the day.

"John (gofer), please go get my mail."
"John, please pass out those papers."
"John, please take this next door."
"John, please take this to the office."
"John, please bring me the answer sheets."

# The Johnny Bianco Show

In many classes, one may find the class clown who spends a great deal of time entertaining his or her classmates. This often-creative distraction requires a great deal of time and teacher attention. You "join the resistance" by telling Johnny that he can have five minutes of time before lunch or dismissal for his comedy routine provided that he does not disturb instruction during the day/period. The show's frequency and participants can be adjusted to your unique setting.

"And now, ladies and gentlemen, I'm proud to present the comedy styling and antics of Johnny Bianco!"

# Desist Commands

| | |
|---|---|
| **What?** | *Desists* are an effective strategy for helping students who are exhibiting minor forms of misconduct. |
| **Why?** | Desists get students back on-task with a minimum of fuss. They are positive prompts (verbal and nonverbal) that are used to inform students of what they should be doing or not doing. |
| **How?** | Follow the techniques below. |

## Mild Desists

1. Clear throat and give the laser stare (NO teacher words).

2. Use corrective visual cues. (See Topic 36.)

3. Use whisper (voice) control. (See Topic 44.)

4. Use the "see me after class" technique. (See Topic 47.)

## Harsh Desists

(These have limited use but may be helpful in some situations.)

1. Yell "STOP!" when two students are fighting in the hall.

2. Say loudly "Absolutely not!" when a student is about to throw an object.

3. When a student is in a physically dangerous situation, bark out a command that makes the student aware of the danger and prevents injury.

# How to Help Kids Cope With Bullies

**Talk to the bully and get him on your side.**

**Refuse to give in.**

**Use your brain to find a creative solution.**

**Use humor to work your way out of the problem.**

**Do not fight.**

**Ignore the bully.**

**Walk away.**

**Tell someone in charge.**

**Learn how to defend yourself.**

**Think of yourself as a strong person.**

**Avoid "problem" kids.**

# Ask a Question, Pay a Chip

I'd like to use a chip...

**What?**   This activity deals with the student who is constantly at your side asking question after question.

**Why?**   This high-need student immensely enjoys talking with/to you. With a classroom of students, however, it is often difficult to spend every minute with one student. The "ask a question, pay a chip" technique limits the contact the student has with you, gives the student reasonable access to you, and allows for your positive acceptance of the student.

**How?**   Say something like this: "Arnold, I really enjoy helping you and that's what I'm here for. However, there are lots of other students in this class and I need to help them, too. So, here's what we are going to do. Every day I'm going to give you six chips (the number is your option and can change with the day or student). Every time you ask me a question, you have to give me a chip. When your chips are gone, you cannot ask any more questions for that day."

**Note:** Unused chips may be used for a reward. See "Pick a Card, Any Card" (Topic 35).

# Handling Conflict

| | |
|---|---|
| **What?** | This topic will assist you in handling feelings of frustration, anxiety, and aggression that often surface in the classroom. |
| **Why?** | To be effective, you need to be capable of handling conflicts that will inevitably be part of the school year. Lead the group to set and reach reasonable goals. |
| **How?** | Meet with the group to: |

1. Set the guidelines for discussion.

2. Clarify what happened.

3. Explore differences in points of view.

4. Identify the causes of the conflict.

5. Develop agreements regarding the cause(s) of the conflict and the resolution of the conflict.

6. Specify a plan of action.

7. Make a positive appraisal of group efforts.

# Cadence

| **What?** | *Cadence* is the measure or beat of your voice. |
| **Why?** | By changing the cadence of your voice, you can send a clear message to students that their behavior is inappropriate and must stop. |
| **How?** | Change your voice cadence by slowing down your speech and emphasizing your words. |

"You . . . will . . . not . . . throw . . . that!"
"I . . . am . . . dead . . . serious!"
"You . . . may . . . want . . . to . . . rethink . . . that . . . choice!"

# SECTION 7

# Teaching Skills

This section contains numerous tips and suggestions for improving instruction. Motivated, on-task students cause a minimum of discipline problems. Many of the included one-minute strategies deal with creating active learners, kids who are alert and thinking. This section is filled with practical, concrete procedures that will enhance your teaching skills and decrease behavior problems.

Good teaching
is one-fourth
preparation
and three-fourths
pure theatre.

GAIL GODWIN

# Dwelling (Going On and On . . .)

| | |
|---|---|
| **What?** | *Dwelling* is spending too much time giving directions, explanations, or details. |
| **Why?** | Dwelling invites off-task behavior. Many students are bored or placed in a passive, or unreceptive, learning mode. |
| **How?** | Avoid dwelling by including as much active student participation as possible. Adopt a rhythm that is sensitive to class attentiveness; as you "read" the group, you are able to adjust your teaching tempo as required. |

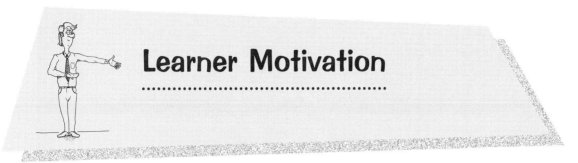

# Learner Motivation

Has your teaching lost some of its zip? Do your students seem to lack motivation? Then take a look at the following.

Interest

## Does your teaching:

- have meaning for students?
- utilize a variety of approaches (large and small group instruction, cooperative learning)?
- actively involve your students?

Level of Concern

## Do you raise or lower anxiety as needed?

*Raise*

"You have seven minutes remaining."

"This information will be on the test."

*Lower*

"You have plenty of time remaining."

"On this assignment, work with a partner."

Success

## Is student work at the correct level of difficulty?

- Neither too hard nor too easy.
- Pre-test.
- Short tasks and small bites.
- Challenging material that a student believes he or she can accomplish.

Rewards

## Are your rewards:

- intrinsic (work hard at this)?
- extrinsic (easy to do)?
- sincere?

Knowledge of Results

## Key ideas here include:

- constructive criticism
- sandwich technique
- immediate feedback

Feeling Tone

## Culture of Appreciation

- Do you really "know" each student?
- Positive relationships.
- Good relationships and "good" times outnumber "bad" times.

# Jerkiness

....................

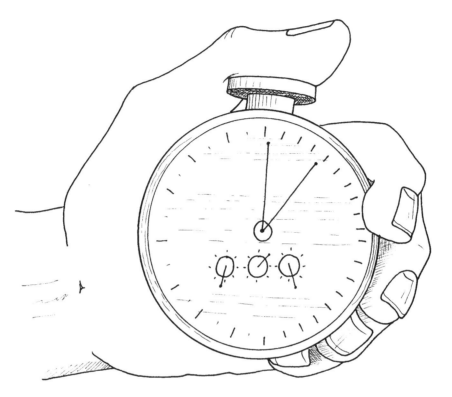

MATH - 17 seconds

Science - 18 seconds

Spelling - 12 seconds

| | |
|---|---|
| **What?** | *Jerkiness* is the failure to move smoothly from one activity to another. |
| **Why?** | Lack of smooth transitions results in time off-task, confusion, noise, delay, and misbehavior. |
| **How?** | Control transitions by planning well and making the class very aware of the time spent between activities. Reward the class with praise, points, etc., for smooth transitions. Transition training is an excellent "procedure + practice = routine" activity (see Topic 19). |

# Thinking Word(s)

A word (or words) that you may repeat from a few times to many times during a lesson is called a "thinking" word. It is used as a momentary "pause" while you collect your thoughts before continuing to speak. You may not be aware of this bad habit, but in most cases it can be easily broken. Thinking words include: "um," "uh," and the ever popular "okay."

### Breaking the Habit

A really good plan involves using the class.

TEACHER:   I have this habit that I need your help to break. I don't know if you've noticed but I say the word "okay" quite a bit when I speak to you. Here comes your job. Every time I say "okay," I want you to raise your hands.

**Note:**   This exercise raises your level of awareness as to how often you use the word. After a short period of time, the "thinking" word frequency is drastically reduced or eliminated. The kids also think this is a fun idea.

# Visual Learners

One way to build self-reliance in the classroom is training students to find the information they need on their own. This increases their ability to function without your constant direction. You are able to conserve important energy while you promote student independence.

The key to success is for you to provide visual support information throughout the classroom and in your lessons.

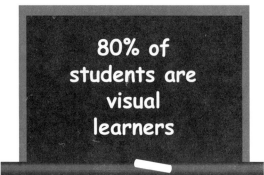

SUPPORT IDEA

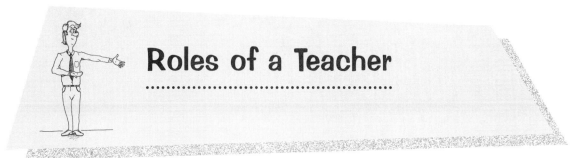

# Roles of a Teacher

The teaching profession presents many instructional challenges. Successful teachers examine a particular classroom situation and adjust their participation as needed. Traditional chalk-and-talk teaching is only one of many instructional models.

**Lecturer**
Conveys information
**Expert Resource Person**
Shares information
**Facilitator**
Guides learning

**Media Expert**
Leads discussions
**Laboratory Supervisor**
Hands-on instruction
**Programmer**
Computer-assisted instruction

**Counselor**
Listens to learners
**Meeting Leader**
Directs activities
**Tutor**
One-to-one instruction

The secret
of teaching
is to appear
to have known
all your life
what you learned
this afternoon.

ANONYMOUS

# Sane Messages

**What?**  *Sane messages* label the kind of behavior and cooperation that you expect of your students.

**Why?**  Sane messages reinforce positive student behavior and work habits. They catch kids being good, invite cooperation, and promote a classroom culture of appreciation.

**How?**  Use such talk as the following:

- "I appreciate the way you return to the room."
- "I can always count on you to be responsible on a trip or when we have a guest."
- "This group has just clearly demonstrated its maturity. We all laughed at that incident and then you responsibly returned to your work. Very nice. Congratulations!"
- "I really like the way you entered the room and began your board-work. Give yourself a pat on the back."

# Words of Praise

# Subject Matter/Discipline Checklist

......................

| | |
|---|---|
| **What?** | The *subject matter/discipline checklist* illustrates the importance of making sure your teaching is not inviting student misbehavior. |
| **Why?** | If instructional material does not meet certain criteria, students will be unchallenged, restless, frustrated, irritable, and in search of causing trouble. |
| **How?** | Refer to the checklist below and keep your "with-it-ness" gauge on constant alert. |

### Possible student reactions:

☐ Subject matter is too easy.  unchallenged; searches for other outlets

☐ Subject matter is too difficult.  frustration, aggression, restlessness, and "I don't care" attitude

☐ Teacher language is too remote from the developmental level of the student.  feels out of place and protests

☐ Assignments are too heavy.  seeks revenge by misbehaving

☐ Assignments are too light.  unmotivated because of lack of progress

☐ Assignments are poorly planned.  irritation and resentment lead to off-task behavior

☐ Work is too infantile.  frustration and off-task behavior

☐ Work is merely on a verbal level.  restlessness, noise, falling off chair

☐ Work is poorly scheduled.  exhaustion and fatigue

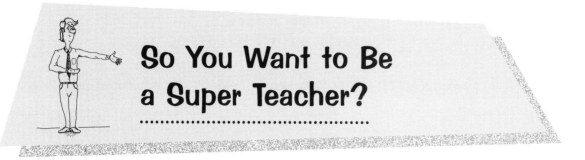

# So You Want to Be a Super Teacher?

Here's the list!

| |
|---|
| **Knowledge of Child Growth and Development** |

| |
|---|
| **Knowledge of Content** |

| |
|---|
| **Classroom Management Skills** |

| |
|---|
| **Planning Skills** |

| |
|---|
| **Instructional Skills** |

| |
|---|
| **Human Relations Skills** |

| |
|---|
| **Knowledge and Use of Materials** |

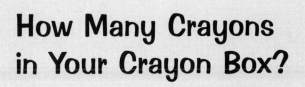

# How Many Crayons in Your Crayon Box?

## Which profile best fits you?

**8?**

- Chalk-and-talk teaching (lecture only—with students very passive).
- Very little visual reinforcement.
- Diminished interest in grade level or subject matter.
- Low on enthusiasm.
- New year, same old stuff.

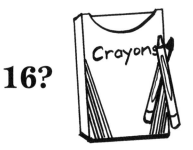

**16?**

- More visual reinforcement (approximately 80% of kids are visual learners).
- Chalk-and-talk teaching, and small and large group activities.
- Increased comfort level with planning and instructional techniques.
- Feeling really good about this grade level and kids.
- Begins seeking out ways to stay fresh and current.
- Begins local visits to other classrooms.

**64!!!** (with the sharpener in the back)

- Many examples of visual reinforcement and word pictures (you have created a collection of visual treats for the students).
- The classroom is your milieu, a very comfortable place to be. You are a rabbit in your very own briar patch!
- Variety of instructional approaches including lecture, small and large groups, cooperative learning, one-on-one, team teaching, tutoring, and self-paced. You know exactly when to change the system.
- Many visits to other classrooms in and out of home school.
- Attends workshops, conferences, and classes to update skills and to keep current. Subscribes to periodicals.
- Shares ideas and works with other teachers in team situations on a new project or a special activity.
- Changes grade levels or assignments to maintain enthusiasm and a positive spirit.
- Active students are on-task and held accountable.

Life is like
a ten-speed
bicycle,
most of us have
gears
that we never use.

CHARLIE BROWN

# Your Modus Operandi

The dictionary definition of *modus operandi* is "a method or procedure." You also have a modus operandi when dealing with students in your classroom. The traditional procedure is that students raise their hands and you call on someone. If done with no variation, this becomes BORING. Student interest wanes and off-task behavior is increased. You become "predictable" and students know they can mentally drop out or create problems.

You must become unpredictable. How? Here are some suggestions:

1. Keep all students on the "hot seat" all the time. Vary your modus operandi so that students can't accurately read you—they must attend.

2. Refer to Topic 61's Support Idea, Roles of a Teacher, for specific techniques, and gradually work these ideas into your instructional program. You will see definite improvement in pupil attention and on-task behavior.

3. "Sweating brains" means just that. Let your students "stew" a little.

   "Is the teacher going to call on me?"

   "I have to listen to the teacher or speaker because I will be held accountable."

   "I have to think more critically because I will be asked to expand on previous statements."

# Teacher Self-Assessment One: The Duck-Ometer

**What?** The *Duck-Ometer* is a visual representation of what you look like when you are in complete control of the class.

**Why?** Kids are excellent at "reading" you. If students observe "weakness" (smaller ducks above), managing behavior and instruction will be negatively affected. "If it looks like a teacher and walks like a teacher, IT MUST BE A TEACHER!"

**How?** Visualize yourself as the large duck (above). Develop:

- A firm, fair, and friendly attitude.

- A "business face" demeanor the first day of the school year and when you begin formal instruction. You might say, "Please prepare for formal instruction." The students then commence (instruction standards) to clear their desks, sit up, and look directly at you.

- A competence in your subject area(s). If you "know your stuff," you exude confidence and stature in the eyes of the students. You are a BIG duck.

*POWER PERCEIVED IS POWER ACHIEVED!*
*How do you rate yourself?*

# Teacher Self-Assessment Two: Sweating Brains

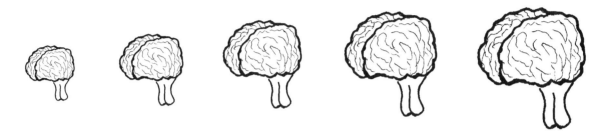

**What?**   The *sweating brains scale* (above) is a visual representation of how effective you are in keeping each student on the "hot seat," alert, listening, and on-task.

**Why?**   Sweating brains keep students in an active learning mode. Kids are required to overtly and covertly participate in the learning process. There is a minimum of daydreaming and off-task behavior.

**How?**   Follow these suggestions:

1. Make transformations, not transactions. (See Topic 78.)

2. Master the technique of "all of the students, all of the time." (See Topic 79.)

3. Build self-reliance by "extracting" from your students rather than "telling." Expert teacher-questioning skills pull (from within) information from students, who then "discover" the learning for and by themselves.

4. Answer a question with a question or request.

   "You tell me."          "Take a risk. What do you think?"
   "Go for it."            "You have a great brain. Use it."

5. Have several students repeat the assignment, worksheet, project, etc., before releasing them to commence work. (See Topic 79.)

# Teacher Self-Assessment Three: Feeling Tone

**What?** The *feeling tone scale* (above) is a visual representation of how effectively you have established a positive learning environment.

**Why?** Students are most inclined to put forth effort to learn if they find the learning situation pleasant and if they anticipate they will be successful.

**How?** Rate yourself on the above scale based on the following characteristics and statements of a positive feeling tone:

| Characteristics | Teacher statements |
|---|---|
| Encouraging words | "You follow directions so well." |
| Encouraging facial expressions | "Thanks for picking that up." |
| Pleasant voice | "You were very polite." |
| Awareness and attention to individuals | "I put a lot of pressure on you and you handled it well!" |
| Student-centered room environment | "You have a clear understanding of that concept." |
| Physical reassurance (pat on the back, high five) | "Your perseverance paid off." |
| Eye contact with a pleasant facial expression | |
| Positive expectations | |
| Praise and compliments | |

# With-it-ness

| **What?** | *With-it-ness* is your ability to know what's going on in all areas of the room at all times. |
|---|---|
| **Why?** | If kids understand that you are on top of all situations, the misbehavior will be nipped in the bud and not spread throughout the group. |
| **How?** | Follow these suggestions: |

1. Anticipate problems and address them ASAP.

2. "Have eyes in the back of your head." "See" the whole class and respond proactively to potential problem incidents.

3. Sense student interest is waning. Then use techniques (see Topic 63) to raise anxiety and interest.

4. Abandon the lesson and move to another activity, or provide a short "break" for the students and then resume the lesson.

TOPIC 68

# Higher-Level Thinking Skills

| Application | Analysis | Synthesis | Evaluation |
|---|---|---|---|
| apply | examine | combine | judge |
| compute | categorize | rearrange | select |
| operate | graph | create | support |
| show | chart | develop | prioritize |
| solve | organize | pretend | justify |
| experiment | discriminate | design | criticize |
| | outline | invent | debate |
| | compare and contrast | compose | recommend |

**What?**   Higher-level thinking skills (Bloom's Taxonomy) enable you to promote and develop critical-thinking skills in students.

**Why?**   Beginning teachers characteristically begin instruction asking lower-level thinking skills (knowledge and comprehension questions). As these teachers gain experience, they are able to add higher-level thinking skills to their repertoires.

**How?**   Place the important terms/verbs (listed above) on cards or a laminated sheet and then put them on a clipboard or with your plans. Refer to the list as you formulate questions throughout the lesson. As you develop the habit of beginning your questions with the key verbs, you will rely less and less on the cards.

"<u>Justify</u> your position in terms of that statement."
"<u>Select</u> the main causes of his decision."
"<u>Recommend</u> your action in regard to her dilemma."
"<u>Examine</u> his motives for not going to the authorities."

# Smoothness and Momentum*

| | |
|---|---|
| **What?** | *Smoothness* is moving students from one activity to the next and *momentum* is regulating the flow and pace of a lesson or activity. |
| **Why?** | Off-task behavior is discouraged when your lesson flows and it uses a minimum of transition time (smoothness). |
| **How?** | Use the checklist below. |

☐ Make students aware of transition time. Verbally praise students for moving quickly from task to task. "That transition took the class less than two minutes. Great work! Give yourselves a pat on the back."

☐ Avoid "rabbit trails" where students or you take the class along a path away from the main objectives of the lesson.

☐ Avoid starting another activity and returning to the original activity.

☐ Don't spend an inordinate amount of time explaining and giving directions. Be brief and specific in giving directions. Monitor the group and use the echo technique to assure that students understand the task at hand.

*Terms by Jacob Kounin, author of *Discipline and Group Management in Classrooms*

# Transition Time

Transition time is the time it takes to move from one activity to another.

## Goals:

- To spend a minimum amount of time in moving from one subject area to another.
- To maximize time for academic instruction.
- To efficiently move from one area of the classroom or building to another.

## Procedures:

1. Hold a class meeting and discuss the importance of quick and quiet transitions.
2. Hold "dry runs" on a regular basis to practice the transition procedures until they become automatic routines.
3. Use your "business face" to stress the importance of this matter.
4. Praise students individually and collectively for reaching a classroom goal for transition time.
5. Tie transition time to bonus recess minutes for a win–win scenario.
6. Use your teacher talents to create more good ideas.

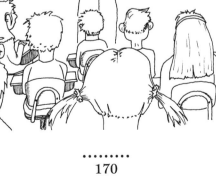

Today, we are going to break the class record for transition time!

# Realness, Acceptance, and Empathetic Listening*

I feel your pain and I will give you more time to complete the test...

**What?**    Realness, acceptance, and empathy are essential attitudes if you are to have maximum effect in facilitating learning.

**Why?**    Students strive to do their very best if there is a positive interpersonal relationship with you. These rapport-building strategies also assist you in managing student behavior.

**How?**    Realness

1. You are genuine, a real person with feelings.
2. You express enthusiasm and boredom.
3. Students feel they can relate to you.

Acceptance

1. You view each student as a person of worth.
2. You view each student as trustworthy.
3. Students feel respected and therefore self-worth is enhanced.

Empathy

1. You are sensitive to students' feelings.
2. The students feel that you understand their feelings.
3. Healthy student–teacher interpersonal relationships promote a positive classroom climate, minimize discipline problems, and promote significant learning.

*Terms by Carl Rogers, author of *Freedom to Learn*

TOPIC 71

# Reality Therapy*

**What?**  William Glasser's reality therapy asserts the idea that the single basic need students have is the need for identity.

**Why?**  "Success" in school is achieved when you develop the students' social responsibility and feelings of self-worth.

**How?**  Follow these suggestions:

1. Accept the student and indicate a willingness to help the student solve the behavior problem.

2. Get a description of the student's behavior problem.

3. Focus on what the student is doing to contribute to the problem.

4. Help the student plan a better course of action.

5. Guide the student to make a commitment to a better course of action.

6. Reinforce the student as he/she follows and keeps the commitment.

7. Accept no excuses if the student fails to follow through on the commitment and alert the student of the need for a better plan.

8. Allow the student to suffer the natural and realistic consequences of misbehavior while helping to develop a better plan and student commitment to it.

*Term by William Glasser, author of *Control Theory in the Classroom*

# Class Meetings*†

**What?**  *Class meetings* are a forum where students discuss any group problem.

**Why?**  Without group assistance, students tend to evade problems, depend on others to solve their problems, or withdraw.

**How?**  Follow these guidelines for meetings:

1. Any group member problem may be discussed; a problem may be introduced by a student or you.

2. The discussion should be directed toward solving the problem.

3. The discussion atmosphere should be nonjudgmental and nonpunitive.

4. The solution should not include punishment or fault finding.

5. The meeting should be conducted with you and the students seated in a tight circle.

6. Meetings should be held often and not exceed 30 to 45 minutes, depending on the age of the students.

*Term by William Glasser, author of *Control Theory in the Classroom*
†See also Topic 13, using class meetings for getting to know your "clients."

If you want
true power,
you must
give some
of it away.

UNKNOWN

# Time Stretchers

·····································

**What?**   *Time stretchers* are verbal encouragement from you reminding the class that the conclusion of the period or activity is at hand.

**Why?**   At the conclusion of a lesson or session, there appears to be a slight loss of student interest and/or attention. You might call it a "sugar low" where students' focus starts to wane. Time stretchers boost and sustain interest through the final minutes of the session.

**How?**   Make a time-notification announcement to the class. For example:

"You people are doing just great! We have about eight more minutes to go. Hang in there."

"I appreciate your hard work. We're coming up on lunch in about seven minutes."

"Thirteen minutes to go. The end is in sight!"

"I really want to compliment you on your effort in working with me on this information. It's pretty heavy stuff and you're handling it very well. Six minutes and you are free!"

·········

# Mentor Teacher

**What?**   Every new teacher should be assigned a veteran mentor teacher.

**Why?**   The mentor teacher has a wealth of background experiences. This "episodic knowledge" will assist the new teacher in dealing with and solving challenging discipline dilemmas. The mentor teacher can also be a source of information on school policies, alternative solutions to problems, and advice on dealing with parents and problem students.

**How?**   The mentor teacher assignment can be made in a formal or informal fashion. It can be mandated or established informally between teachers. The mentor teacher should also observe the new teacher and offer valuable assistance in developing teaching and classroom-management skills.

# Paraphrasing

| | |
|---|---|
| **What?** | Paraphrasing is a student restatement of a concept or of a statement made by you. |
| **Why?** | The student's restatement of the topic of discussion or important information increases attentiveness and listening skills. |
| **How?** | Randomly (or by using techniques under Topic 79) call on students as follows: |

- **Echo:** A restatement (of what was said) in the same words.
- **Simple:** A restatement in student's own words.
- **Translation:** A restatement using very different words without changing the meaning.
- **Summary:** A restatement that captures the meaning of a long communication in a much shorter form.

Students are alert and listening because at any time they may be called on to restate as directed by you (using **echo, simple, translation,** and **summary**).

| | |
|---|---|
| TEACHER: | What was one of the major causes of the American Revolution? (Wait time) Charlie? |
| CHARLIE: | (Charlie gives answer.) |
| TEACHER: | **ECHO** (Wait time) . . . Martha? |
| MARTHA: | (Repeats answer.) |
| TEACHER: | Very good. **SIMPLE** (wait time) . . . John? |
| JOHN: | (Restatement in his own words.) |

**Note:** Paraphrasing is an excellent review technique. The pacing/tempo of the review should be rapid, keeping all students on the "hot seat."

## All of the Students, All of the Time

This technique requires that all students listen to the speaker. In order to respond, elaborate, and summarize, all students must be concentrating and on-task.

| Teacher: | Student: |
|----------|----------|

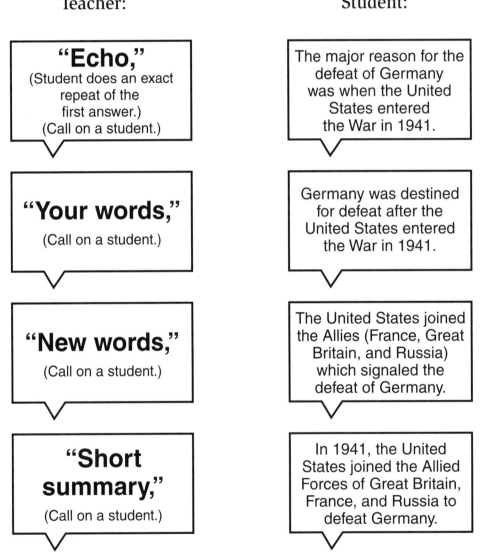

**"Echo,"**
(Student does an exact
repeat of the
first answer.)
(Call on a student.)

The major reason for the
defeat of Germany
was when the United
States entered
the War in 1941.

**"Your words,"**
(Call on a student.)

Germany was destined
for defeat after the
United States entered
the War in 1941.

**"New words,"**
(Call on a student.)

The United States joined
the Allies (France, Great
Britain, and Russia)
which signaled the
defeat of Germany.

**"Short
summary,"**
(Call on a student.)

In 1941, the United
States joined the Allied
Forces of Great Britain,
France, and Russia to
defeat Germany.

# Wait Time

Wait time is the length of time you pause after asking a question. Extended wait time is the length of time you wait after a student comments or asks a question.

**A minimum of 3 to 5 seconds is recommended.**

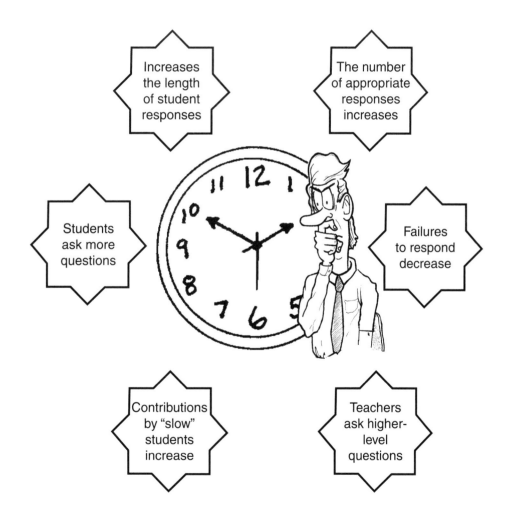

Increases the length of student responses

The number of appropriate responses increases

Students ask more questions

Failures to respond decrease

Contributions by "slow" students increase

Teachers ask higher-level questions

# Hurdle Help

| **What?** | *Hurdle help* is a teacher prompt that enables students to get over the first "barrier" and motivates them to attack the next challenge. |
|---|---|
| **Why?** | When the student is at an impasse, the learning process comes to a halt. Hurdle help encourages the student to try again and thereby creates achievement momentum. |
| **How?** | Use prompts, adapting them to the subject and situation. |

- "Let me help you with that one. Now let me see you do one. Very good. Now do two more and bring them to me to check." (Student does two more and brings them to you.)

- "Very good! Now complete the row and bring it to me." (Student completes the row and returns to you.)

- "Excellent! You are ready to complete the assignment."

# Cross-Age Tutors

Upper-grade students can very effectively serve as tutors for younger students. Many lower-grade teachers follow their "graduates" and recruit them for tutoring duty.

**Tips:**

1. Provide a training session for your tutors to discuss their duties, do's and don'ts, confidentiality issues, and schedules.

2. Recruit enough helpers so that you do not pull tutors an inordinate amount of time from their home classrooms, which are their first obligation.

3. Match your "needy" kid(s) (academic and discipline) with your top tutors.

4. Provide a study area in your room or in the hall for students to work.

5. Schedule a thank-you party for your tutors during the year.

6. Secondary students are an excellent source of classroom assistance. Certain secondary classes require students to work with students at a lower level. Connect with an upper-level colleague to establish a program and schedule.

# Skills for Constructive Criticism

**What?**   *Skills for constructive criticism* are techniques for positively motivating students to do their very best work.

**Why?**   The more positive techniques and ideas that you are able to acquire, the more students will grow and improve.

**How?**   Follow these constructive criticism recommendations:

1. Criticize in private as much as possible.

2. Give suggestions when you are *not* angry, insulted, or wronged.

3. Condemn the sin, *not* the sinner.

4. Avoid the word *you.*

5. Give the student a chance to be heard.

6. Let the offender suggest a remedy. (See Topic 32.)

7. Insist the student make a commitment to change. Offer your support.

8. Don't change the subject or soften the impact of the criticism. This often decreases the gravity of the infraction. You want the impression to "stick."

# Transformations, **Not** Transactions

| | |
|---|---|
| **What?** | *Transactions* (3,000 a day) give the students a fish. *Transformations* (self-reliance) teach students to catch their own fish. |
| **Why?** | Transformations teach students to use their own brains. They keep students in an active mode, always on the "hot seat" and with "sweating brains." |
| **How?** | Become more of a facilitator and less of a lecturer. View yourself as a conductor, *not* a soloist. |

| Soloist: Less active | Conductor: More active |
|---|---|
| 1. "With this card and these blocks we are going to . . ." | 1. "I'm going to show you a card and some blocks. What do you think we are going to do?" |
| 2. Call on a student and ask a question. | 2. Ask a question. (Wait time.) Call on a student. |
| 3. Student gives an answer and you repeat it. | 3. Student gives an answer and you call on another student to repeat it. "Tell us what Sara said . . . John." "Rephrase Michael's answer for us . . . Mia." |
| 4. Student requests information and you respond with an answer. | 4. Answer a question with a question or request. "You tell me." "Take a risk . . . I know you know it." Student answers and then teacher praises. "Great thinking!" "Outstanding!" "Bingo!" |
| 5. "You have some sentence strips on your desks. What I want you to do is . . ." | 5. "Knowing what you now know, what do you think we will do with these sentence strips?" |
| 6. "At the top of page 10 is a box, and what your assignment is . . ." | 6. "At the top of page 10 is a box. Who can tell me what you are going to do?" Student gives information . . . another repeats . . . another repeats (last time) and it's now safe to have the students start the assignment. |

# Be a Conductor, Not a Soloist

> *Education is not the filling of a pail, but the lighting of a fire.*
>
> —WILLIAM BUTLER YEATS

**Great Conductor Lines!**

If you don't go out on a limb, you'll never get any fruit.

You tell me.

What do you think? I know you know it.

Take a risk!

Knowing what you now know, what happens next?

Now what do you think we are going to do?

# All of the Students, All of the Time

| | |
|---|---|
| **What?** | *All of the students, all of the time* includes a number of techniques and procedures that you use to keep all students thinking and on the hot seat. |
| **Why?** | All of the students, all of the time requires that all students have "sweating brains," i.e., these students must be on-task, awake, and thinking. |
| **How?** | Use a *variety* of questioning techniques that require all students be tuned in at all times. It is important that you be unpredictable as to which technique you might use. This forces the students to remain alert at all times. |

| Questioning Technique | How? |
|---|---|
| 1. Students raise hands | 1. Your traditional call on student for the response/answer. |
| 2. Sweat box | 2. Place each student name in a box and draw a name to answer the question. |
| 3. Echo technique | 3. Call on a student and then ask another student to repeat the answer, and then another student to rephrase the previous answers. |
| 4. Scanner | 4. Pose a question and then use your index finger and wait time to point to a random student to answer. |
| 5. Choral response | 5. Ask questions and then twirl index finger in a circle to signal the class that you want a choral (total group) response. |
| 6. Student to student | 6. Call on a student who answers the question and then poses another question to another student . . . and so on. |

> **Keep the pace moving!**

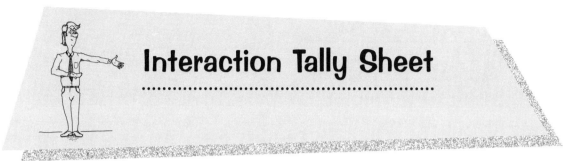

# Interaction Tally Sheet

Interactions between you and students occur many times throughout the school day. Interactions can be either positive or negative. Here are examples of each:

| Positive Interactions | Negative Interactions |
|---|---|
| "Great thinking, Shelly." | "How many times do I have to tell you?" |
| "I can always count on you." | "Why aren't you finished?" |
| "Charlie, you are a great thinker." | "Keep your hands to yourself." |
| "Right on target." | "I've told you to stay away from him." |
| "What a great kid!" | "Your talking is very annoying." |
| "Super effort! Give yourself a pat on the back." | "Stay in your seat." |
| "Excellent! Pick a reward card." | "No way. Not in this class." |

The interaction tally sheet provides you with information such as:

How often do you call on each individual student?
Are some students passed over on a regular basis?
Are the more able students receiving more interactions?
Are your interactions of a positive or negative nature?
Are "problem" kids receiving an inordinate amount of your time?

Designate an aide to tally the interactions on a class list (below). The tallier must be briefed as to what constitutes a negative or positive interaction. The purpose of the tally sheet and confidentiality of the tally information is shared with the tallier. Review the results and adjust your interactions and discussion techniques as needed.

| September 14–28 | | |
|---|---|---|
| Students | Positive | Negative |
| Debbie | IIIII | II |
| Julie | III | IIIII II |
| Caitlin | IIIII I | I |
| Peter | II | III |
| Joe | IIIII III | IIIII |
| Arnoldo | IIII | IIIII II |
| Virginia | III | IIII |

# Ripple Effect

**What?**  The *ripple effect* is accomplished by verbally praising individuals or small groups in an effort to motivate the entire class.

**Why?**  This positive reinforcement technique will send the proper message to the rest of the class and motivate them to conform to the highlighted good behavior or teacher-reinforced work habits.

**How?**  Use statements such as the following:

- "I can see that several people have already completed half their work . . ."
- "Table four people are all completed."
- "John already has four sentences."
- "Very responsible work, group two."
- "I can always count on you to know what to do next."

SUPPORT IDEA

# Early Finisher Chart

The early finisher chart is a must for every effective classroom. As you know, work completion varies greatly among students. The early finishers are reminded and directed to positive ways to spend this "extra" time.

1. With the class, list the free-time possibilities on the chalkboard.
2. Transfer the list to a chart and display it.
3. Review the chart information with the students.
4. Have a dry run. "Let's see what the class would look like if you all were doing an activity listed on the chart. Ready, go!"
5. Have individual students tell what they are doing.
6. Start the plan and positively reinforce students on a regular basis.

### Early Finisher Ideas

1. Help a friend.
2. Go to reading center.
3. Do homework.
4. Go to game center.
5. Complete DOL, DOM, DOG. (Daily Oral Language, Math, Geography)
6. Complete other assignments.
7. Study for next test.
8. Go to listening center.
9. Silent reading time.
10. Complete journal writing.
11. Study for spelling test.
12. Complete work on your project.

# SECTION 8

# Great "Little Gems"

This section covers a wide range of "little gems." The range of eclectic topics includes: establishing a token economy plan, a test review idea, a plan to delegate a routine task to students, and an excellent idea for surveying (prior to the start of a unit) students' background knowledge.

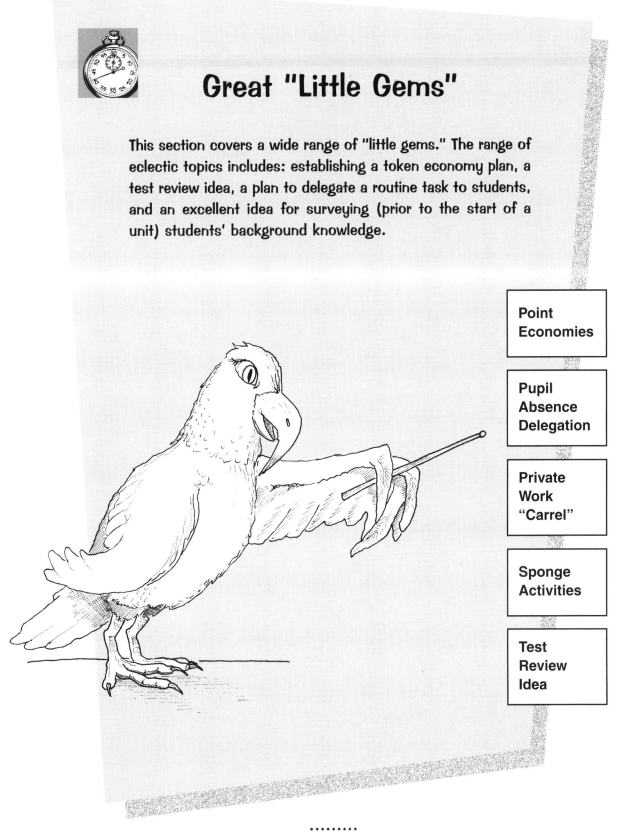

Point
Economies

Pupil
Absence
Delegation

Private
Work
"Carrel"

Sponge
Activities

Test
Review
Idea

# Student–Teacher Communication Ideas

**What?**  *Student–teacher communication ideas* are tips for easing and facilitating communication between students and you.

**Why?**  There are many positive benefits for you, including the following:

- These provide an orderly method of responding to student requests and questions.

- The written communiqué (see below) eliminates many of the less important or trivial inquiries and therefore saves you time and energy.

- The visual ideas allow you to scan the class and easily see who needs assistance.

**How?**  Follow these suggestions:

1. Red and blue plastic cups are glued together and placed on each student's desk. If the student needs help, he or she turns the cups so that the red one is on top.

2. The students who need assistance list their names on the board. You can visually see each name and then proceed to the student's seat to administer assistance.

3. Each student has a folded sign on his or her desk. The sign says "Help Me" on one side and "Keep Working" on the other. The student turns the "Help Me" sign to the front when help is needed.

4. (*my personal favorite*) The student writes a detailed note to you requesting assistance and places it in the note box. When you are free, you read the note(s) and are then able to respond to each request.

# Sticky Notes

Maintaining the classroom as a culture of appreciation requires that you visibly promote and reinforce positive work habits and behavior. How? Follow these steps:

1. Acquire a supply of sticky notes.

2. Whenever possible, jot down a quick note to each student. The note is placed on the student's desk or books.

3. Include positive strokes for work completion, effort, and good behavior.

Make this kind of "roving" behavior a daily habit. It requires a very short expenditure of time.

Many teachers recount stories of kids who cherish their notes, placing them on bedroom walls or refrigerators.

Parents also respond favorably to the personal attention their children receive.

# Token (Point) Economies

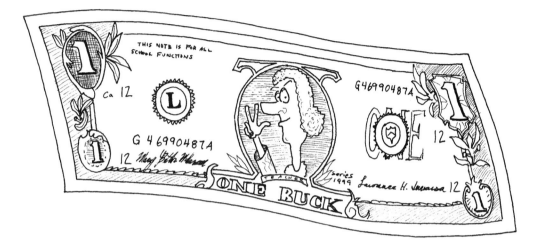

| | |
|---|---|
| **What?** | Many teachers use a "point system" as a universal medium of exchange to reward acceptable behavior. |
| **Why?** | Point systems put a positive spin on the activities in a classroom or school. They reinforce character development (see below), are enjoyed by students, and can be used to promote positive relationships throughout a school. |
| **How?** | Give the "points" in the form of tokens, chips, stars, marbles, check marks, "dollars," etc. The points are then exchanged for a large variety of rewards including popcorn parties, movie tickets, points on tests, computer time, trinkets, "goodies," chitchat time, etc. Point systems often have a short lifespan. After several weeks, the system begins to fade, so the activity should be modified or concluded and saved for a future time. |

(Back of "dollar")

_____ has earned a dollar for:

___ Honesty    ___ Special service    ___ Caring attitude    ___ Academic excellence

___ Politeness    ___ Citizenship    ___ Helpfulness    ___ Consideration of others

___ Reasoned argument    ___ Respect for others    ___ Knowledge    ___ Integrity

___ Freedom of thought & action    Signed _____

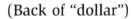

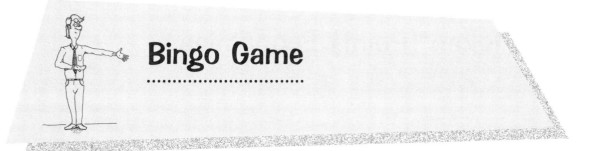

# Bingo Game

Here's a sample Bingo board to use with your students. One Bingo (across, down, vertical, or any other shape specified) equals 20 minutes of computer time (or a reward of your choice).

**How to use:** The student brings the Bingo game to you at the end of a period or morning/afternoon session. The student can recommend a particular square that he or she has accomplished or completed during that session. If you agree, an X is placed on that square. The student can also bring the Bingo chart to you at regular intervals for positive reinforcement. When the student completes a Bingo, he or she receives the computer time or another reward. The Bingo squares can be adjusted or changed based on the individual student or a specific class.

| B | I | N | G | O |
|---|---|---|---|---|
| I respond to requests the first time. | I am a good sport during a game. | I don't interrupt my classmates. | FREE | I always speak clearly. |
| FREE | I use an inside voice. | I seldom complain. | I never whine in class. | I respond to requests the first time. |
| I come to class with homework completed. | I participate in class discussions. | FREE | I cooperate with my teacher. | I am responsible for my own behavior. |
| I am a good class citizen. | I respect other students' possessions. | I am polite and considerate of others. | I have a good sense of humor. | FREE |
| I clean-up after myself and others. | FREE | I assist a friend with his or her work when asked. | I share with my classmates. | I make progress every day in class. |

# Reward Spinner

An excellent idea for promoting a "culture of appreciation" is the use of a reward spinner. The spinner has numbers on it that correspond to pre-numbered class or individual rewards (or the spinner could be large with rewards listed on it). "Catch 'em being good."

Here's how the spinner works:

1. Single out a student for special recognition.

2. Tell the class why the behavior is being rewarded. (This reinforces the behavior.)

3. Allow the student to spin the spinner and call the number. The class or individual receives the payoff.

## Sample payoffs:

- 10 extra recess minutes
- "No homework" pass
- Pizza party
- Special Friday video
- Popcorn party

- 15 minutes of free reading
- Praise note to parents
- Seat of honor for one week
- Line leader (first to lunch)
- 20 minutes of computer time

# Class Aid Box

**What?** Obtain three or four boxes (about double the size of a shoe box) and place a red cross on each box.

**Why?** With the use of class aid boxes, you are able to delegate many classroom responsibilities (worksheets/tests/assignments for absent students, parent newsletters and reminders, notes and schedule changes, etc.). You save valuable time having students do these housekeeping tasks. This also promotes class cooperation and consideration for classmates.

**How?** Model a "dry run" using a class aid box. Share a sample box with the class as well as the procedure for stuffing the box.

# Student Offices

**What?** Student offices are cardboard trifold dividers that make each pupil seat into a study carrel. Each student can decorate his or her own "office."

**Why?** The student offices provide privacy for each student. The dividers can be used during a test, to provide a private reading area, and to focus student attention away from distractions and on the task at hand.

**How?** Ask the students to bring in cardboard trifolds or acquire them from a store or moving company. The trifolds should fit each desk and then fold easily to be placed beside the desk so they take up minimal space. The trifolds measure approximately 18 in. (side) by 24 in. (back) by 18 in. (side) by 18 in. (height).

When you want them in place, say, "Please put up your offices."

Students who require a minimum of distractions will definitely benefit from this idea. **Caution:** Do not use the offices for punitive action. They should be a positive learning tool for students.

# Sponge Activities

The illustration shows a teacher pointing to a board that reads:

*Daily oral language*
*Two sentences –*
*1. I lost the directions to Tucson.*
*2. Are we there yet?*

| | |
|---|---|
| **What?** | *Sponge activities* are "filler" activities that take anywhere from a few minutes to 15 minutes. |
| **Why?** | Every minute of the day is valuable time. Sponge activities maximize the learning time for each student. |
| **How?** | Create a file of sponge activities, which can include: |

- Board work (a 5- to 7-minute review activity when students enter the classroom)
- DOL, DOM, or DOG (Daily Oral Language, Daily Oral Math, Daily Oral Geography, commercial chart activities that can be purchased at a teaching tools store or from a catalog)
- Review worksheets and parts of past tests
- Review material from previous lesson(s)
- Board games
- Drill exercises

# Exit/Entrance Questions

**What?**  An *entrance question* is asked as the students enter the room. An *exit question* is a one-on-one (teacher–student) question at the close of a period, before lunch, or before dismissal.

**Why?**  These questions are an excellent way to review the lesson material just presented or material from recent lessons. This technique also increases listening skills because the students know they will have to answer a question before they are released.

**How?**  Have students line up at the door and ask each one a question related to a recent lesson or today's lesson or unit. Students who give correct answers are (depending on your class/school rules and procedures) free to go, OR they may return to the classroom for social (chitchat) time. Students who give incorrect answers go to the rear of the line and must wait for another question.

# Bell Work

· · · · · · · · · · · · · · · · · · · · ·

✔ Today's Assignments

1. Name the seven dwarfs.

2. Alphabetically list the capitals of the 50 states.

3. Write a 7,000-word essay on the meaning of life.

| | |
|---|---|
| **What?** | *Bell work* is an assignment that the students begin immediately at the beginning of the period or after they enter the room in the morning. |
| **Why?** | Bell work sets the tone for the period/day. It provides structure to any classroom and minimizes socializing and goofing off. Bell work is also an excellent tool for review and reinforcement of previously taught material. |
| **How?** | Designate an area of the board for the daily bell work assignment. The actual bell work can be delegated to an aide, another student, or can be taken from a commercially prepared workbook available at a teaching tools store. |

# The Tattle Box

**What?** The *tattle box* is an excellent idea for eliminating or minimizing tattling.

**Why?** *Tattling* is a source of frustration and a waste of valuable instructional time.

**How?** Prepare the tattle box (a shoe box with a slit in the top) and require tattlers to do the following:

1. Write down exactly what happened to you.

2. Describe the problem in full detail in a paragraph including your name, date, and time of the event.

3. Younger children can be asked to draw a picture of what happened and an aide or study buddy can assist with the writing. **Note:** The writing requirement will eliminate many of the trivial problems that arise on the playground or in the classroom.

4. You can now:
   a. individually handle the written complaints, *or*
   b. empty the tattle box on Friday and address the dilemmas in a group problem-solving session

**Note:** During the meeting, many kids will forget the issue by Friday, thereby eliminating trivial or resolved problems. Further problems can also be eliminated by having the tattle period as part of a recreation or special activity time that the kids really enjoy. This will limit the discussion of trivial matters.

# Clipboard Record Sheet

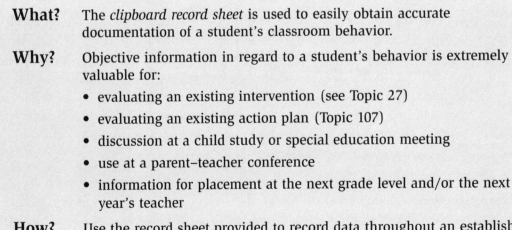

| N = Not working | T = Talking |
| D = Disturbing neighbors | F = Not following directions |
| O = Out of seat | I = Incomplete work |

| | Name | Date | Date | Date | Date | Date | Date | Date | Date |
|---|---|---|---|---|---|---|---|---|---|
| 1 | | | | | | | | | |
| 2 | | | | | | | | | |
| 3 | | | | | | | | | |
| 4 | | | | | | | | | |
| 5 | | | | | | | | | |
| 6 | | | | | | | | | |
| 7 | | | | | | | | | |
| 8 | | | | | | | | | |
| 9 | | | | | | | | | |
| 10 | | | | | | | | | |
| 11 | | | | | | | | | |
| 12 | | | | | | | | | |
| 13 | | | | | | | | | |
| 14 | | | | | | | | | |
| 15 | | | | | | | | | |
| 16 | | | | | | | | | |
| 17 | | | | | | | | | |
| 18 | | | | | | | | | |
| 19 | | | | | | | | | |
| 20 | | | | | | | | | |
| 21 | | | | | | | | | |
| 22 | | | | | | | | | |
| 23 | | | | | | | | | |
| 24 | | | | | | | | | |
| 25 | | | | | | | | | |
| 26 | | | | | | | | | |
| 27 | | | | | | | | | |
| 28 | | | | | | | | | |
| 29 | | | | | | | | | |
| 30 | | | | | | | | | |

**What?** The *clipboard record sheet* is used to easily obtain accurate documentation of a student's classroom behavior.

**Why?** Objective information in regard to a student's behavior is extremely valuable for:
- evaluating an existing intervention (see Topic 27)
- evaluating an existing action plan (Topic 107)
- discussion at a child study or special education meeting
- use at a parent–teacher conference
- information for placement at the next grade level and/or the next year's teacher

**How?** Use the record sheet provided to record data throughout an established recording period.

# Clipboard Record Sheet

N = Not working                T = Talking
D = Disturbing neighbors       F = Not following directions
O = Out of seat                I = Incomplete work

| | Name | Date | Date | Date | Date | Date | Date | Date | Date |
|---|---|---|---|---|---|---|---|---|---|
| 1 | | | | | | | | | |
| 2 | | | | | | | | | |
| 3 | | | | | | | | | |
| 4 | | | | | | | | | |
| 5 | | | | | | | | | |
| 6 | | | | | | | | | |
| 7 | | | | | | | | | |
| 8 | | | | | | | | | |
| 9 | | | | | | | | | |
| 10 | | | | | | | | | |
| 11 | | | | | | | | | |
| 12 | | | | | | | | | |
| 13 | | | | | | | | | |
| 14 | | | | | | | | | |
| 15 | | | | | | | | | |
| 16 | | | | | | | | | |
| 17 | | | | | | | | | |
| 18 | | | | | | | | | |
| 19 | | | | | | | | | |
| 20 | | | | | | | | | |
| 21 | | | | | | | | | |
| 22 | | | | | | | | | |
| 23 | | | | | | | | | |
| 24 | | | | | | | | | |
| 25 | | | | | | | | | |
| 26 | | | | | | | | | |
| 27 | | | | | | | | | |
| 28 | | | | | | | | | |
| 29 | | | | | | | | | |
| 30 | | | | | | | | | |

# The Raffle Jar

| | |
|---|---|
| **What?** | The *raffle jar* is used to reward and reinforce positive behavior and work habits in the classroom. |
| **Why?** | Effective teachers send a clear message to students that they will be rewarding and reinforcing acceptable behavior and habits. The raffle jar also assists in creating a positive classroom environment that promotes the mental health of both the students and the teacher. |
| **How?** | Throughout the week, catch the students doing something positive; for example, workers who are on-task, helping others, remembering important information, following a routine, being a good class citizen, etc. Reward the students with a ticket. The student puts her or his name on the ticket and places it in the jar. The more tickets a student has in the jar, the more chances he or she can win. On Friday, draw the winner(s) and give any number and type of reinforcer. |

# Beanbag Review

| **What?** | *Beanbag review* is a fun activity used to review material before a test. You can also use this action activity for reviewing material after new instruction. |
|---|---|
| **Why?** | Students respond to a variety of approaches that make learning fun. |
| **How?** | Ask the class a question, pause (wait time), and then throw the beanbag to a student. The student answers the question (or not) and then returns the bag to you. Use creative variations, such as student to student, at your discretion. |

**Note:** As in any new activity of this kind, it is important to establish clear expectations for appropriate behavior during the activity. This activity will be strengthened if it is used sparingly throughout the year. "Always leave 'em wanting more."

# The Big Brain Poster

**What?**  The *big brain* is a large laminated poster that can be placed on the chalkboard or easel.

**Why?**  The poster is used to assess prior knowledge at the beginning of a lesson or unit. It can also be used for review before a test.

**How?**  Introduce a new unit or topic to the class. For example: "Today, we begin our unit on the Renaissance. On your desk you have a sticky note. Please briefly write a statement about something that you already know about the Renaissance." Students record the information on the sticky note and then come to the board and place it on the Big Brain poster. You can also ask the students to explain their information to the class.

# Survival Skills

This section provides you with information for conserving valuable energy throughout the school year. These ideas will assist you in not only maintaining endurance, but also providing relief from negative influences and stresses that are part of every classroom.

# Mentor Teacher*

**What?** Every new teacher should be assigned a veteran mentor teacher.

**Why?** The mentor teacher has a wealth of background experiences. This "episodic knowledge" will assist the new teacher in dealing with and solving challenging discipline dilemmas. The mentor teacher can also be a source of information on school policies, alternative solutions to problems, and advice on dealing with parents and problem students.

**How?** The mentor teacher assignment can be made in a formal or informal fashion. It can be mandated or established informally between teachers. The mentor teacher should also observe the new teacher and offer valuable assistance in developing teaching and classroom-management skills.

*See also Topic 74, having a mentor help with your teaching skills.

Two are better than one

for if they fall,

one will lift up his fellow,

but woe to him that is alone

when he falleth,

and hath not another to lift him up.

ECCLESIASTES

# Pickles and Cucumbers

Beginning teachers are faced with a number of challenges their first year.

These fresh, snappy, new "cucumbers" are immediately confronted by the incumbent "pickles" (who often hang out in the teachers' lounge). The goal of the negative "pickles" is to "corrupt" the new recruits and create more "pickles." They may say such things as:

"You can tell he's new."

"You won't be like that next year."

"Wait until you've been here awhile."

"I tried that years ago and it didn't work."

"That's not the way it's done around here."

"Let me tell you about her."

"It's the (pick one) media, principal, parents, weather, district office, other teachers, that is the problem."

## Snappy answers for beginning cucumbers:

"I'm new here, I really don't know anything about that."

"Maybe you should talk directly to her."

"I appreciate your experience and advice and I'll let you know how it goes."

"I really value your opinion, but I'll have to see for myself."

"If it works, I'd be more than happy to share it with you."

"We can get together with the other people and work it out."

"I know it can be a jungle out there, but our mission is to be here for kids."

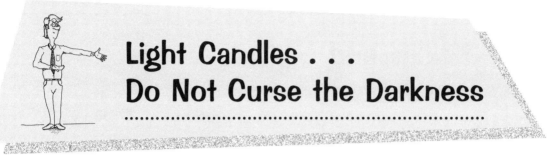

## Light Candles . . .
## Do Not Curse the Darkness

It is extremely important to keep a positive attitude throughout the school year. You may get worn down by the "pickles" or other stressful aspects of the job. To guard against these negative influences, it is recommended that you focus on: the progress of a particular student; an upcoming trip; a new exciting activity; or a successful lesson, unit, or field trip. Share your good news with your mentor, a friend, or just smile on the way out that day and say, "I did very well today."

**"Blake had a great week! He has made marked progress since September."**

**"Martha, I just received new materials from my docent friend. I'd love to share them with you."**

**"Mrs. White is a great parent aide. She is always reliable and a great assistant."**

**"This is the class from heaven. We are having a great year."**

**"Our principal is very supportive. She quickly responded to my concerns."**

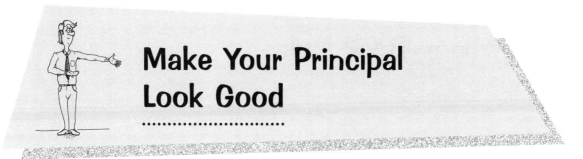

# Make Your Principal Look Good

1. Do something during the year to make your principal look good to other teachers, students, parents, or the superintendent.

2. Learn what frustrates your principal and help eliminate the frustration.

3. Go to your principal armed with a solution to a problem.

4. Keep your principal informed.

5. Praise (when warranted) your principal to others.

6. Take good care of your "clients," namely, students and parents.

7. Find new ways to solve problems, save money, and do things better.

# Taking-Back Rule

| | |
|---|---|
| **What?** | This *rule* finds you "taking back" or reestablishing order in your classroom. |
| **Why?** | As the year progresses, you often (gradually) lose more and more control. Draw a line in the sand. Order must be reestablished. |
| **How?** | "Take back" your classroom by following this procedure: |

1. Get a good night's sleep.

2. Put on your "business face" and go to school ready to act.

3. Reestablish your dominance of the class. You are the alpha dog!

4. Assertively review rules and establish a zero tolerance policy toward any transgressors.

**Note:** The *taking-back rule* can be implemented at *any* time during the year. It is particularly effective if all teachers adopt the strategy schoolwide.

# Your Physiological and Emotional Condition

| **What?** | You must be fully aware of how you physically feel when a stressful or challenging situation occurs. There are many days when you have tremendous patience, while on other days patience is a thin veneer. |
|---|---|
| **Why?** | You must be careful on the days when your patience is at a premium. Rash statements or punishments made when you are not at your best will often come back to haunt you. |
| **How?** | Invoke the 24-hour rule. (See Topic 96.) Often the next day the mountain is no more than a molehill. "I think it would be best to discuss this situation tomorrow. Let's plan to meet at 9:30." |

**The best bridge between hope and despair is a good night's sleep.**

# The 24-Hour Rule

**What?** The *24-hour rule* dictates that you delay any action or decision for one day.

**Why?** Emotionally charged situations often provoke poor decisions and even major mistakes. The 24-hour rule gives everyone an opportunity to cool down and better assess the situation and the options. *"The bridge between hope and despair is often a good night's sleep."*

**How?** Possible statements you might say are:

- "I'm pretty upset right now and I would like to put this on hold and meet you the first thing in the morning."

- "I feel that you're upset right now, so why don't we both give this some thought and I'll call you first thing in the morning."

- "We are having a difficult time with this, so I promise I will call you tomorrow to review the dilemma."

- "Before making a rash decision, why don't we give this some thought and we will meet with you at 8:00 A.M."

# Small Victories

**What?** Small victories enable you to realistically assess student progress during the year.

**Why?** Challenging students may show dramatic change or growth, but all too often growth is made in "baby steps." If you are aware that your interventions and hard work are paying dividends, the small victories ("looking on the bright side") become excellent encouragement.

**How?** If there is a feeling of frustration with pupil progress or what is perceived as lack of progress, refer to the student's individual progress folder (Topic 105) and *dated* anecdotal information. In most cases, you'll find that progress ("baby steps") is being made. You, the student, and parents can now share in a victory celebration. This is good mental health information if you are frustrated with what is perceived as a lack of progress. If progress is not being made, new interventions (Topic 27) are required.

Questions to consider:

- Is the student less disruptive than he or she was four months ago?
- Does the dated anecdotal information note progress?

TOPIC 98

# Handling Hostility

**What?** On occasion, you are confronted by a hostile student or parent.

**Why?** Being able to handle a hostile situation is an excellent survival skill for teachers.

**How?** See the checklist below for suggestions on ways to diffuse hostility.

## Hostility Checklist

☐ Get the upset person to a private area. ("Step in here and we can talk.")

☐ Carefully reflect by using a pad to take notes. If that irritates the person, tell him or her that a copy of the session will be given.

☐ If the person is speaking loudly, request that he or she "speak more slowly." If you ask the person not to yell, he or she may become more irritated. "Please speak more slowly. I can help you better if I know what the problem is."

☐ Validate the person and/or the problem. Paraphrase the problem and say "I can see how you would be upset about that."

☐ Listen by rephrasing and reflecting the person's concerns.

☐ "Fess up" if you are at fault. "When you bow, bow low." People do make mistakes.

☐ State: "This will not happen again."

☐ Ask directly: "What would you like me to do?"

☐ Formulate options and alternatives with parent input.

☐ Evaluate alternatives and explanations.

☐ Document the meeting with a copy to the parents.

☐ Make and keep follow-up commitments (phone call, another meeting, letter, etc.).

**Note:** If possible, get information and assistance from another teacher or last year's teacher(s).

# Breaking Up a Fight

| | |
|---|---|
| **What?** | In the event of a fight, this information gives you a plan of action. |
| **Why?** | Although breaking up a fight is an infrequent occurrence, it is always a good idea to be prepared. |
| **How?** | Follow this suggested plan: |

1. Get help. Send a student for another teacher, office help, etc.

2. Dismiss the audience. Order students away from the incident or out of the area.

3. Identify yourself as a person in authority.

4. Identify the aggressor and concentrate your attention on him/her. (Use broken-record technique, Topic 48.)

5. Direct the nonaggressor away from the scuffle to a specific location.

6. Obtain identification (if not in your class).

7. Make a written report as per school policy.

8. After the dust settles, debrief with students involved.

# Crisis Management

........................................................

| | |
|---|---|
| **What?** | On rare occasions, you may be confronted by a student or parent who is in crisis and/or out of control. |
| **Why?** | Crisis management equips you with valuable knowledge and techniques to use when faced with a person's irrational behavior. |
| **How?** | See the crisis-management plan outlined below. |

## Teacher Do's:

1. Remain calm.
2. Use a respectful tone and volume of voice.
3. If possible, isolate the person(s).
4. Set limits. (Calmly assert what the person *cannot* do.)
5. Be aware of nonverbals (anxiety and stress).
6. Attempt to listen.

## Teacher Don'ts:

1. Panic or overreact.
2. Get into a power struggle.
3. Fake attention.
4. Ignore.
5. Threaten.
6. Personalize.

## Verbal Escalation Pattern of Person Out of Control

The person will:

- Phase 1. Question and challenge your authority.

  *Teacher response:* Answer any questions and remain calm and rational. Redirect if possible.

- Phase 2. Refuse your direction or suggestion (noncompliant behavior).

  *Teacher response:* Restate (clearly and concisely) what the person can and cannot do.

- Phase 3. Have an emotional outburst (verbal venting).

  *Teacher response:* Allow to vent and isolate if possible.

- Phase 4. Attempt to intimidate or threaten you or someone else.

  *Teacher response:* Take all threats seriously and calmly repeat what the person cannot do.

- Phase 5. Begin to reduce his or her tension/stress level.

  *Teacher response:* Assist the person with problem solving and resolution.

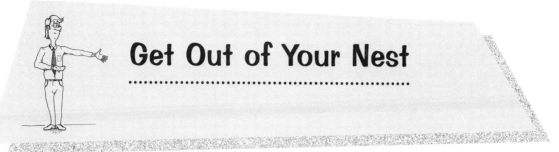

# Get Out of Your Nest

One of the most important ways to update your skills, pick up new ideas, and stay current is to get out of your classroom and visit other teachers and schools. Sure, your little nest is comfortable and secure, but growth requires that you be exposed to new methods and different ways of doing things.

Teachers tend to be isolated, which has a narrowing effect on what they do. Professional growth and stimulation is promoted by personally relating to what other teachers are accomplishing. Most teachers are very comfortable in sharing materials, ideas, and plans. Teachers are excellent at begging, borrowing, and friendly stealing!

# ADHD Information

Students with ADHD (attention deficit hyperactivity disorder) are said to exhibit a combination of these behaviors over a period of several months.

- Is easily distracted by their environment
- Misplaces school assignments, books, toys
- Makes careless mistakes in schoolwork
- Has trouble paying attention to details
- Struggles with concentrating on one activity at a time
- Moves around the classroom in a disruptive fashion
- Impulsively responds to questions
- Apparently does not listen, even when addressed directly
- Is easily distracted by activity around them
- Talks constantly, even at inappropriate times
- Fidgets and squirms constantly

Is Ritalin® an answer to ADHD problems? Here is some current information on Ritalin®:

1. Ritalin® appears to help in the short term, but no long-term research regarding academic performance or social behavior is available.

2. Ritalin® appears to be a safe drug that may cause insomnia and may interfere with or stunt growth rates.

3. Ritalin® is not a panacea.

4. Treating students who are not attending or daydreaming remains a challenging problem.

5. Brain research is unclear as to pinpointing a biochemical defect in students with ADHD.

6. Nutritional research holds some promise for treating students with ADHD.

7. There has been an increase in prescriptions for children under the age of 5.

8. More research is needed.

# Balanced and Weighted Classrooms

Each year teachers and principals meet to establish class lists for the new year. There are many systems that attempt to make the process more "scientific" and thereby create "balanced" classrooms. The goal of a "balanced" classroom is to make all the sections of that grade level as heterogeneous and as teachable as possible.

The concept of weighted classes is important. The following methods of placing students can always be adapted to individual schools and grade levels.

## Method 1

1. Place students' names on 4 by 6 colored cards.

2. Devise a system of placement, for example:

   • Blue cards = above average ability
   • Yellow cards = average ability
   • Green cards = below average ability
   • Red cards = discipline problems
   • White cards = special education or other unique problems

   (Categories and placement criteria are totally optional.)

3. Sending teachers may then meet with the receiving teachers and/or the school principal to place the students.

4. "Balanced" classes would theoretically have an equal number of "challenges" in each section.

5. Parent input may be taken into consideration at the option of each school.

## Method 2

1. Assign a "weight" to students in various categories.

   1 = above average
   2 = average
   3 = below average
   4 = discipline problems
   5 = special education students

   (Again, categories, numbers, and placement criteria are totally optional.)

2. Students are placed so that each section receives a similar "total" number of students.

# Forms

This section provides a number of time-saving forms that you can photocopy and use as is or adapt to meet your particular needs. They range from a "Substitute Teacher Feedback Form" to action contracts (interventions). The classroom–office forms provide an excellent way to promote teacher–principal communication.

# Substitute Teacher Folder

**What?** A folder with important information can be used by the substitute teacher.

**Why?** Substitute teachers need all the help they can get. The substitute teacher folder provides vital information for a smooth-running and instructionally beneficial day.

**How?** Purchase substitute teacher folders at any teaching tools store (or prepare one of your own). Include information on:

- Daily schedule
- Extra teacher duties
- Class rules/procedures
- Where to find stuff
- Map of school
- Special class schedules
- Special student schedules
- Attendance procedure
- Lunch procedure
- Fire drills
- How to reach office/principal
- Dismissal procedure
- Group information
- Hall passes

# Substitute Teacher Feedback Form

........................................

| | |
|---|---|
| **What?** | The *substitute teacher feedback form* establishes clear expectations for student behavior in the absence of the regular teacher. |
| **Why?** | This form helps to achieve the maximum amount of educational benefit when the regular teacher is absent. A tremendous amount of instructional time is lost due to misbehavior of students with substitute teachers. |
| **How?** | Review the form provided with students the first week of school. "The substitute teacher is a guest in our classroom and will be treated with respect. 'Super stars' **and** 'fallen stars' will be rewarded or dealt with upon my return." Leave the form on your desk (in the substitute teacher folder, Topic 101) each night before leaving school. |

# Substitute Teacher Feedback Form

Dear Substitute: Please complete at the end of the day. Thank you.

1. Were the lesson plans adequate for the day?   ___Yes ___ No

2. Student behavior:  ___ Excellent  ___ Good  ___ Needs Improvement  ___ Poor

   **Super Stars?**                **Fallen Stars?**

   _____           _____

   _____           _____

3. Complete and corrected work can be found: _____
   _____
   _____

4. The thing I liked best about this classroom: _____
   _____
   _____
   _____
   _____

5. My teaching would have been more effective if: _____
   _____
   _____
   _____
   _____

Comments _____
_____
_____
_____
_____
_____
_____

                          Signed _____

                          Date _____

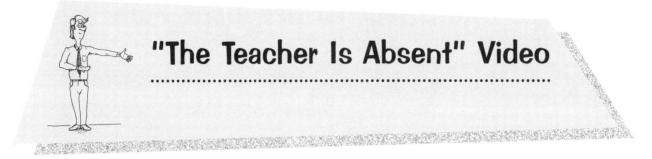

## "The Teacher Is Absent" Video

Record a tape for use when you are absent. The substitute teacher pops the tape in the VCR and the class can watch you share important information and instructions.

# Office Discipline Ticket

| **What?** | The *office discipline ticket* facilitates communication between the classroom teacher and the office/principal. This form should be a specific color. |
|---|---|
| **Why?** | When a student is sent to the office, the student often tells only his/her side of the story and frequently paints the teacher as the real villain. The office discipline ticket tells the principal or assistant principal the real story behind the ejection from class. The form also enables you to forward information and recommendations. |
| **How?** | Take a minute to calm down (a good idea because *calm is control*) and complete the form provided. The student returns to class with the office part of the form completed. The form becomes part of the student's personal folder. |

# Office Discipline Ticket

Student _____ Date _____

Teacher/supervisor_____ Time _____

**Reason:**

____ Disturbing class            ____ Inappropriate language

____ Throwing object(s)         ____ Class-rule infraction

____ Inappropriate movement    ____ Temper tantrum

____ Fighting                      ____ Hurting classmate(s)

____ Cafeteria behavior         ____ Work not completed/student defiant (send work)

____ Other _____

**Teacher Recommendation:**

____ Discipline action ticket

____ Office timeout   ___ 5 minutes   ___10 minutes   ___15 minutes   ___30 minutes
                          ___ lunch recess

____ Parent conference (with student/teacher/principal)

____ Teacher/student/principal conference

____ Serious reprimand

------------------------------------------------------------

**Office to Return to Classroom with Student**

____ Action plan completed and attached      ____ Work completed

____ Timeout served                        ____ Call made to parents
      (isolation in office—minimal
      contact with others)

____ Offender reprimanded                 ____ Parent conference scheduled

Office signature _____ Time _____

Comments:

_____

_____

_____

_____

# Discipline Action Ticket

**What?** The *discipline action ticket* is a form completed by the student who has broken an important rule. It is similar to a speeding ticket for an adult. It is also an information form that reviews life skills that are valued in this school or classroom.

**Why?** The ticket is an excellent written review of the rule infraction or student misbehavior. Without a written record, signed by all parties, the facts of the "incident" may become fuzzy and open to speculation. The written word carries more weight and clarifies any future misinterpretation. The ticket is excellent documentation for future disciplinary action or for referral for testing or placement in special education.

**How?** Have the student complete the form provided in writing. (Younger students may dictate the answers.) The student and you sign the form, and you complete the comments area (if necessary). Send the form to parents for signature(s) and then file, with a warning to the student of the future consequences connected with another "strike."

**Note:** This form can also be adapted for use between classroom and home. Office (principal) participation is certainly advantageous, but not an absolute necessity.

# Discipline Action Ticket

Name _____  Room # _____

Teacher _____  Date _____

    This action ticket is designed to assist you in solving your problems using LIFE SKILLS taught at our school. Your parent or guardian will review this form with you. Then return it to school.

| | | | | | |
|---|---|---|---|---|---|
| integrity | patience | initiative | flexibility | perseverance | friendship |
| responsibility | sense of humor | effort | caring | problem-solving | |
| organization | curiosity | cooperation | common sense | | |

**In your own words:**

1.  What happened? (What did I see, hear, or feel?)

_____

_____

2.  What do I believe caused this to happen?

_____

_____

3.  What was my part in what happened?

_____

_____

4.  What LIFE SKILLS (listed above) could I have used in this situation?

_____

_____

5.  What will I do next time?

_____

_____

**Comments from teacher/adult/monitor:** Write these on the back of this action ticket.

Student signature _____ Date _____

Parent signature _____ Teacher signature _____

☐ Strike 1.  Student–teacher or student–principal conference (no parent notification).

☐ Strike 2.  Parent signature required before student returns to school.

☐ Strike 3.  Student/parent/teacher or principal conference required.

☐ Strike 4.  In-house suspension; Circle:  2 hrs.  4 hrs.  all day  ___ days

☐ Strike 5.  Suspension: _____ days

# Student Information Folder

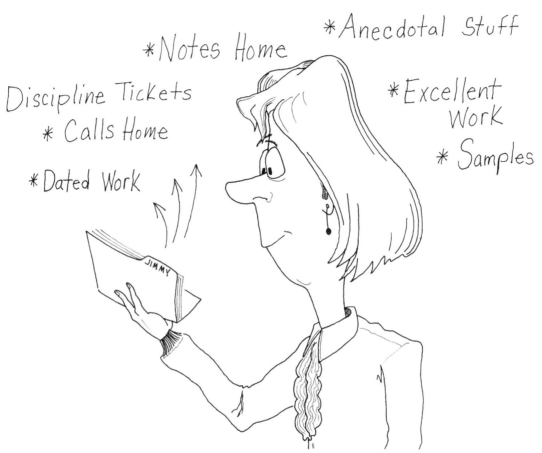

**What?**   You maintain a *student information folder* on each student in the classroom. The folder contains a variety of information, such as: a representative sampling of *dated* examples of the student's academic work, any forms relating to discipline (discipline action tickets), copies of notes or calls to parents, and reports from other teachers.

**Why?**   This folder is an outstanding tool for reporting progress to parents and documenting the pupil's work profile for the school principal, counselor, or special education purposes. The folder can also be used to counsel with individual students or the class as a whole throughout the year to reinforce their excellent work and progress.

**How?**   Establish the folder the first week of school and delegate folder maintenance (stuffing) to a responsible student or aide. Folders are present at parent conferences or at any meeting concerning the student. Folders can then be forwarded to the student's next teacher.

# Daily Schedule

## MORE

\*reading alone
\*reading with
 someone
\*playing sports

## Less

\*T. V.
\*eating
\*sleeping

**What?**    The *daily schedule* represents the student's life after school hours.

**Why?**    It is very important to understand what activities the student is
participating in when *not* at school. Is the student watching too much
T.V.? Is there a regular time for homework each night? What is the
student's work schedule? Do parents agree (or even know) about the
schedule? etc.

**How?**    Establish individual conferences with each student to review each
schedule (see form provided) and make suggestions/recommendations
to the student and/or parents. Parents may be asked to sign the
completed schedule at the annual "Meet the Teacher Night." Completed
schedules can be compared and reviewed at conferences or if an
academic problem surfaces.

# My Daily Schedule

**Monday** _____ (date)

3:00 _____ 7:00 _____

4:00 _____ 8:00 _____

5:00 _____ 9:00 _____

6:00 _____ 10:00 _____

**Tuesday** _____ (date)

3:00 _____ 7:00 _____

4:00 _____ 8:00 _____

5:00 _____ 9:00 _____

6:00 _____ 10:00 _____

**Wednesday** _____ (date)

3:00 _____ 7:00 _____

4:00 _____ 8:00 _____

5:00 _____ 9:00 _____

6:00 _____ 10:00 _____

**Thursday** _____ (date)

3:00 _____ 7:00 _____

4:00 _____ 8:00 _____

5:00 _____ 9:00 _____

6:00 _____ 10:00 _____

**Friday** _____ (date)

3:00 _____ 7:00 _____

4:00 _____ 8:00 _____

5:00 _____ 9:00 _____

6:00 _____ 10:00 _____

Student signature _____

Parent signature _____ Teacher signature _____

# Student–Teacher–Parent Action Contracts

| **What?** | *Student–teacher–parent contracts* are action plans (interventions) designed to identify areas of concern in regard to student behavior or academic growth. |
| --- | --- |
| **Why?** | These action plans are excellent interventions when student behavior needs to be modified. If you do nothing, nothing will change. |
| **How?** | Identify the main areas of concern for the action plan. Establish a monitoring system requiring participation by you, the student, and the parent. Five different action contracts are provided. Be sure to regularly monitor objective progress, and have action plans become part of the student information folder (see Topic 105). Action plans usually have a particular lifespan that varies with each student. If the plan becomes less effective, you and the parents may vary the reinforcement or "graduate" the student. |

**Note:** The action contracts must be *easy* for the student and you to complete.

# Student–Teacher–Parent Action Contract

Name _____     Date _____

Teacher _____     Grade _____

*Student circles and returns to teacher daily or at the end of the week.*

**Target Areas**
(list as many as needed)

| | Monday | Tuesday | Wednesday | Thursday | Friday |
|---|---|---|---|---|---|
| 1. _____ | Super | Super | Super | Super | Super |
| | OK | OK | OK | OK | OK |
| | Poor | Poor | Poor | Poor | Poor |
| 2. _____ | Super | Super | Super | Super | Super |
| | OK | OK | OK | OK | OK |
| | Poor | Poor | Poor | Poor | Poor |
| 3. _____ | Super | Super | Super | Super | Super |
| | OK | OK | OK | OK | OK |
| | Poor | Poor | Poor | Poor | Poor |
| 4. _____ | Super | Super | Super | Super | Super |
| | OK | OK | OK | OK | OK |
| | Poor | Poor | Poor | Poor | Poor |

Week of: _____     Student signature _____

Teacher signature _____     Parent signature _____

# Student-Teacher-Parent Action Contract

| | On Time | Quiet Worker | Appropriate Behavior | Best Work | Courteous/ Respectful | **Daily Totals** |
|---|---|---|---|---|---|---|
| Monday | _____ | _____ | _____ | _____ | _____ | _____ |
| Tuesday | _____ | _____ | _____ | _____ | _____ | _____ |
| Wednesday | _____ | _____ | _____ | _____ | _____ | _____ |
| Thursday | _____ | _____ | _____ | _____ | _____ | _____ |
| Friday | _____ | _____ | _____ | _____ | _____ | _____ |

Comments _____

_____

_____

_____

_____

_____

_____

_____

Student signature _____ Teacher signature _____

Please sign and return the bottom to your teacher.

- - - - - - - - - - - - - - - - - - - - - - - - - - - - - - - - - - - - - - - - - -

_____'s Contract Action Plan
               (name)

Week of: _____

Parent comments:

_____

_____

_____

_____

_____

_____

Parent signature _____

# Student–Teacher–Parent Action Contract

Student _____    Teacher _____    Week of _____

| Goals | Monday | Tuesday | Wednesday | Thursday | Friday |
|---|---|---|---|---|---|
| 1. Responds to request with no more than one reminder | Yes | Yes | Yes | Yes | Yes |
|  | No | No | No | No | No |
| 2. Attempts every task with a positive approach | Yes | Yes | Yes | Yes | Yes |
|  | No | No | No | No | No |
| 3. Starts and stops work assignments promptly | Yes | Yes | Yes | Yes | Yes |
|  | No | No | No | No | No |
| 4. Refrains from blaming others when having difficulties | Yes | Yes | Yes | Yes | Yes |
|  | No | No | No | No | No |
| 5. Completes assignments in small groups | Yes | Yes | Yes | Yes | Yes |
|  | No | No | No | No | No |
| 6. Interacts with classmates in an acceptable way | Yes | Yes | Yes | Yes | Yes |
|  | No | No | No | No | No |

Comments:

_____

_____

_____

_____

_____

_____

**Signatures**

Student: _____    Date: _____

Teacher: _____    Date: _____

Parent: _____    Date: _____

# Student–Teacher–Parent Action Contract

Name _____     Week of _____

|   |   | Monday | Tuesday | Wednesday | Thursday | Friday |
|---|---|--------|---------|-----------|----------|--------|
| 1. | Listens to teacher | Super<br>OK<br>Poor | Super<br>OK<br>Poor | Super<br>OK<br>Poor | Super<br>OK<br>Poor | Super<br>OK<br>Poor |
| 2. | Listens to classmates | Super<br>OK<br>Poor | Super<br>OK<br>Poor | Super<br>OK<br>Poor | Super<br>OK<br>Poor | Super<br>OK<br>Poor |
| 3. | Stays on-task | Super<br>OK<br>Poor | Super<br>OK<br>Poor | Super<br>OK<br>Poor | Super<br>OK<br>Poor | Super<br>OK<br>Poor |
| 4. | Follows directions | Super<br>OK<br>Poor | Super<br>OK<br>Poor | Super<br>OK<br>Poor | Super<br>OK<br>Poor | Super<br>OK<br>Poor |
| 5. | Out-of-class behavior | Super<br>OK<br>Poor | Super<br>OK<br>Poor | Super<br>OK<br>Poor | Super<br>OK<br>Poor | Super<br>OK<br>Poor |
| 6. | Quality work | Super<br>OK<br>Poor | Super<br>OK<br>Poor | Super<br>OK<br>Poor | Super<br>OK<br>Poor | Super<br>OK<br>Poor |
| 7. | Turns in assignments on time | Super<br>OK<br>Poor | Super<br>OK<br>Poor | Super<br>OK<br>Poor | Super<br>OK<br>Poor | Super<br>OK<br>Poor |

Comments                                    Signatures

_____     Student _____

_____

_____     Teacher _____

_____

_____     Parent(s) _____

_____

_____     Date _____

_____

# Student–Teacher–Parent Action Contract

🙂 If it's to be, it's up to me! 🙂

| What I will do! | Monday | Tuesday | Wednesday | Thursday | Friday |
|---|---|---|---|---|---|
| 1. | S: 🙂 😐 🙁<br>T: 🙂 😐 🙁 | S: 🙂 😐 🙁<br>T: 🙂 😐 🙁 | S: 🙂 😐 🙁<br>T: 🙂 😐 🙁 | S: 🙂 😐 🙁<br>T: 🙂 😐 🙁 | S: 🙂 😐 🙁<br>T: 🙂 😐 🙁 |
| 2. | S: 🙂 😐 🙁<br>T: 🙂 😐 🙁 | S: 🙂 😐 🙁<br>T: 🙂 😐 🙁 | S: 🙂 😐 🙁<br>T: 🙂 😐 🙁 | S: 🙂 😐 🙁<br>T: 🙂 😐 🙁 | S: 🙂 😐 🙁<br>T: 🙂 😐 🙁 |
| 3. | S: 🙂 😐 🙁<br>T: 🙂 😐 🙁 | S: 🙂 😐 🙁<br>T: 🙂 😐 🙁 | S: 🙂 😐 🙁<br>T: 🙂 😐 🙁 | S: 🙂 😐 🙁<br>T: 🙂 😐 🙁 | S: 🙂 😐 🙁<br>T: 🙂 😐 🙁 |

S = Student rating     T = Teacher rating

# Appendix

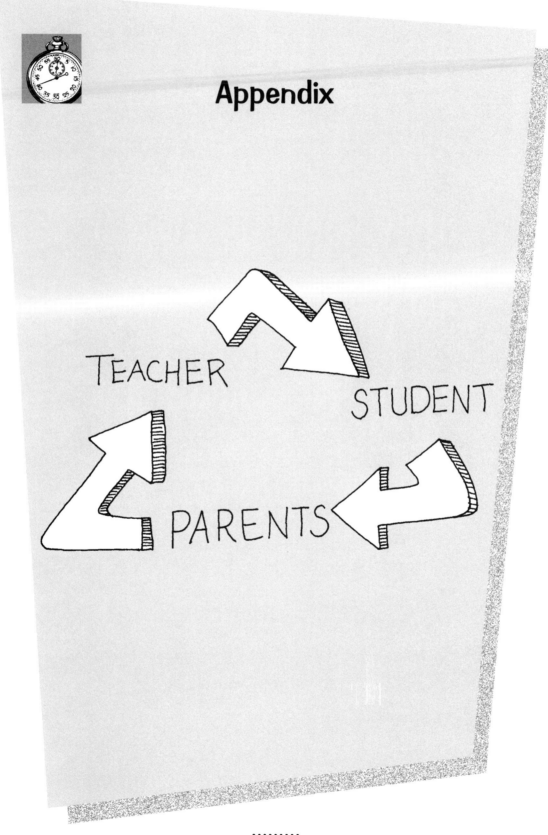

# One-Minute Discipline Self-Check Review

| Give yourself: | Scores |
|---|---|
| 2 points for doing a terrific job | 16–20 = Terrific |
| 1 point for doing an average job | 11–15 = Very good |
| 0 points for needing improvement | 0–10 = Change required |

_____ 1. I consistently look beyond "outside" factors that are out of my direct control when dealing with students. Although frustrating, I don't let the negative influences of home situations, the media, T.V., my principal, my colleagues, or public opinion dictate how I teach each student. I try not to commit any sins of omission.

_____ 2. I understand that each class is a challenging assortment of unique individuals. Some groups create more challenges than others. I readily accept the opportunity to make academic and social progress with each student.

_____ 3. I am aware that progress may not always come in dramatic fashion and that small victories over the course of the year become a positive contribution to the development of each student.

_____ 4. I never do anything I can't delegate to a student. I take the time to train (side by side) students and aides before I assign them to a task.

_____ 5. I am committed to opening the gate of change and thereby begin to change unsuccessful habits and replace them with more effective ones.

_____ 6. I am constantly searching for new ideas, techniques, and strategies that I can add to my repertoire.

_____ 7. I am prevention-centered. I plan in advance and take the time necessary to avoid future problems.

_____ 8. I empower my students by making them use their own thinking skills. I promote self-reliance on a daily basis.

_____ 9. I promote a culture of appreciation in my classroom.

_____ 10. I strive to keep my teaching fresh, creative, and motivating. I seek out new ideas and new ways of doing things.

Curiosity is the very basis of education, and if you tell me that curiosity killed the cat, I say only the cat died nobly.

ARNOLD EDINBOROUGH

# One-Minute Teacher Contributions

I would like to contribute my *one-minute discipline* idea.

Send to: Arnie Bianco, 4475 N. Summerset Drive, Tucson, Arizona 85750.

Name _____

City/District _____

Signature _____ Date _____

**What?** _____

_____

_____

_____

_____

_____

**Why?** _____

_____

_____

_____

_____

_____

**How?** _____

_____

_____

_____

_____

_____

# Bibliography

Bloom, B. S. Time and learning. *American Psychologist*, 1974, 29, 682–688.

Breeden, T. and Egan, E. *Positive Classroom Management*. Nashville, TN: Incentive Publications, Inc., 1997.

Canter, L. and Canter, M. *Assertive Discipline: A Take Charge Approach for Today's Educator*. Los Angeles: Canter and Associates, 1976.

Canter, L. *Back to School with Assertive Discipline*. Santa Monica, CA: Lee Canter & Associates, 1990.

Cooper, J. M. *Classroom Teaching Skills*. Boston: Houghton Mifflin Co., 1999.

Curwin, R. *The Fourth R*. Eau Claire, WI: Otter Creek Institute, 1999.

Dreikurs, R., Grunwald, B. B., and Pepper, F. C. *Maintaining Sanity in the Classroom*. New York: Harper and Row, 1971.

Ginott, H. *Teacher and Child*. New York: Macmillan, 1971.

Glasser, W. *Control Theory in the Classroom*. New York: Perennial Library, 1985.

Glickman, C. D., Gordan, S. P., and Ross-Gordon, J. M. *Supervision of Instruction*. Boston: Allyn & Bacon, 1998.

Johnson, L. V. and Baney, M. A. *Classroom Management: Theory and Skill Training*. New York: Macmillan, 1970.

Jones, F. *Positive Classroom Discipline*. New York: McGraw-Hill, 1987.

Joyce, K. and Weil, M. *Models of Teaching*. Boston: Allyn & Bacon, 1996.

Kauchak, D. R. and Eggen, P. *Learning & Teaching: Research-Based Methods*. Needham Heights, MA: Allyn & Bacon, 1996.

Kounin, J. *Discipline and Group Management in Classrooms*. New York: Holt, Reinhart and Winston, 1970.

Partin, R. *Classroom Teacher's Survival Guide*. Paramus, NJ: The Center for Applied Research in Education, 1999.

Redyl, F. and Wattenberg, W. *Mental Hygiene in Teaching*. New York: Harcourt, Brace and World, 1951, 1959.

Rhode, G., Jenson, W. R., and Reavis, H. K. *The Tough Kid Book*. Longmont, CO: Sopris West, Inc., 1992.

Rogers, C. *Freedom to Learn*. Columbus, OH: Merrill, 1969.

Ryan, K. and Cooper J. *Those Who Can Teach*. Boston: Houghton Mifflin Co., 2000.

Thompson, J., *Discipline Survival Kit for the Secondary Teacher*. Paramus, NJ: The Center for Applied Research in Education, 1998.

Watson, G. *Teacher Smart!* Paramus, NJ: The Center for Applied Research in Education, 1996.

Williamson, B. *Classroom Management: A Guidebook for Success*. Sacramento, CA: Dynamic Teaching Company, 1992.

Wong, H. *The First Days of School*. Sunnyvale, CA: Harry K. Wong Publications, 1991.